WHITE KNUCKLE RIDE

WHITE KNUCKLE RIDE

The illustrated guide to the
world's biggest and best
roller coaster and thrill rides

Mark Wyatt

a Salamander book

Published by Salamander Books Limited
LONDON

A SALAMANDER BOOK

Published by Salamander Books Ltd
129–137 York Way, London N7 9LG,
United Kingdom

© Salamander Books Ltd 1996

10 9 8 7 6 5 4 3 2

Distributed by
Random House Value Publishing, Inc.
40 Engelhard Avenue
Avenel, New Jersey 07001

A CIP catalog record for this book is available
from the Library Of Congress

ISBN 0-517-15945-7

Printed in England

Designer and editor: Paul Johnson
Color Reproduction: P&W Graphics PTE,
  Singapore

Jacket Front Cover: (main picture) Magnum
  XL200, Cedar Point, Sandusky, Ohio; (top
  left) Cyclone, Astroland, Coney Island, New
  York; (center) The Great Nor'Easter, Morey's
  Pier, Wildwood, New Jersey; (bottom) Wild
  One, Adventure World, Largo, Maryland.
Jacket Back Cover: (main picture) Screamin'
  Eagle, Six Flags Over Mid-America, Eureka,
  Missouri; (top left) Canyon Blaster, Circus
  Circus, Las Vegas, Nevada; (bottom left) The
  Pepsi Max Big One, Blackpool Pleasure
  Beach, Lancashire, England; (bottom right)
  Splash Mountain, Walt Disney World, Lake
  Buena Vista, Florida
Endpapers: (front) Nemesis, Alton Towers,
  Staffordshire, England; (back) Predator,
  Darien Lake, Darien Center, New York.
Half Title: Skyrider, Paramount Canada's
  Wonderland, Maple, Ontario, Canada.
Title: Kumba, Busch Gardens Tampa Bay,
  Florida.
Page 4: Serpent Of Fire, La Feria, Mexico City.
Page 5: Structure of Mean Streak, Cedar Point,
  Sandusky, Ohio.

PHOTOGRAPHS
All photographs in this book are by Mark Wyatt,
with the exception of the following:

Don Eiler's Custom Photography, Richmond,
  Virginia: Jacket Front Cover (main picture), 5,
  49, 50 (left), 52–53 (left, right, center bottom)

Paul Johnson: Jacket Back Cover (bottom left),
  10, 21 (top), 31 (right), 87 (top, bottom right),
  91 (top), 101 (top), 107

Alton Towers: Front Endpapers, 91 (left, bottom)

David Wynn, Logansport, Indiana: 8, 41 (both)

TOGO International Inc: 17, 94 (both), 95 (both)

Chessington World Of Adventures, Surrey,
  England: 21 (bottom)

Six Flags Magic Mountain, Valencia, Ca: 23

Lou Ann Shirk: 24

Mark Jencks: 25 (inset)

Busch Gardens Tampa Bay, Florida: 25 (top)

Cedar Point, Sandusky, Ohio: 26;
  Dan Feicht/Cedar Point: 50–51 (center)

Timothy Puetz, Reliable Steel Inc, Las Vegas,
  Nevada: 27 (top right)

Gary Slade: 28–29 (all), 36–37 (both),
  40 (right), 42 (both)

Knott's Berry Farm, Buena Park, Ca: 30 (both)

Paramount's Kings Island, Ohio: 46 (bottom)

John Knight: 54 (bottom)

Busch Gardens Williamsburg,
  Va: 66 (both), 103

West Edmonton Mall, Edmonton,
  Alberta, Canada: 81 (both)

Disneyland Paris: 86 (both)

Blackpool Pleasure Beach: 87
  (main picture)

Lord Lichfield, for Blackpool
  Pleasure Beach: 88–89

Lightwater Valley, North
  Yorkshire, England: 90 (both)

Port Aventura, Spain: 92–93 (all)

Kentucky Kingdom, Louisville,
  Kentucky: 102 (top)

Paramount's Kings Dominion,
Doswell, Va: 104

CONTENTS

Chapter One

A RIDE THROUGH THE YEARS

The number one thrill ride at
amusement parks has always
been the roller coaster. Its origins
can be traced from giant ice
slides in Russia, to coasting
courses in France, and from
there to the early amusement
park scenic railways of the 1900s.
From then on, in every sense,
it has been downhill
all the way...

White knuckle rides come in many forms. In the amusement and theme parks of the world, there are literally hundreds of different types of thrill rides and attractions to choose from, but the undisputed international king of the midway remains the roller coaster. Considering the intense competition for delivering excitement, its longevity is surprising. The roller coaster stood as the centerpiece of hundreds of amusement parks at the turn of the 20th century, and continues to draw the spotlight internationally as the world enters the 21st.

Below: The 1380-foot long Jack Rabbit, at Clementon Amusement Park, New Jersey, is the oldest coaster in the world still operating in its original location. It was built in 1919 by Philadelphia Toboggan Company.

FROM THE BEGINNING

The story of the evolution of roller coasters is filled with almost as many highs and lows, twists and turns as the rides themselves. But one constant throughout history has been the presence of a 'mountain.' Historians have traced the origins of coasters back to the 'Russian Mountains' of the 15th century. Now, more than 500 years later, we are able to travel in excess of 100 miles per hour on a roller coaster at Six Flags Magic Mountain. In the endless search for thrills on hills, no one has yet invented the 'ultimate' ride.

The predecessors of roller coasters were actually sledding hills built in Russia in the 1400s, most notably in the town of St Petersburg. Technically, these tall structures can best be described as ice slides, constructed to keep the locals entertained during the long, frigid Russian winters. The slides were built of wood and sometimes covered with ice and snow. Thrillseeking pioneers would climb up a staircase, board a sled carved from a block of ice and slide down the ramp. The ice slides were usually built in pairs, positioned parallel to each other so that the sled would come to rest at the base of the other slide. The rider could pick up his or her sled, climb the other staircase and repeat the process. Speeding down the wooden ramps in the icy cold winter weather not only provided the Russians with a thrilling pastime, it was also quite cold on their physical extremities, and is possibly the earliest example of a real 'white knuckle' ride.

Over the years, the Russian ice slides became more and more sophisticated, some standing 70 feet tall and spanning several blocks. They would eventually be open to sliders even at night, lit by torches spaced out along the edges of both sides. Known in the 1700s as 'Flying Mountains,' the structures were often decorated with canopies, pagodas, detailed paintings and other ornamental features. As the sleds became more sophisticated, the surfaces of the slides were built from harder wood, and some were even constructed indoors.

In the late 1700s, the town of St Petersburg made history again by becoming the site of the first actual roller coaster utilizing wheels. A device called the Switchback was introduced at the Gardens of Orienbaum, using vehicles with small wheels that ran in shallow grooves down a sloping track with gentle hills. It was during this period of time that rollers were installed in some

Left: Zippin' Pippin was built in Memphis, Tennessee, by National Amusement Device in 1915. It was dismantled, moved and rebuilt, with amendments to its design, in Libertyland, at the Mid-South Fairgrounds, in 1923. The Pippin has a length of 2865 feet and a 70-foot drop.

of the slides, forming a 'conveyor'-type runway and making the sleds slide even faster. Because they were coasting across the rollers, the attractions were logically dubbed 'roller coasters' for the first time.

A few years later, in 1804, another roller coaster with wheels called Les Montagnes Russes (Russian Mountains) debuted in Paris. (Sometimes the wheels stayed on, often they did not). Documented accidents and injuries were frequent, but did not frighten away potential riders. The world was eager to ride.

In 1817, two more roller coasters debuted in Paris, known as 'Les Montagnes Russes a Belleville' (The Belleville Mountains) and 'Promenades Aeriennes' (Aerial Walks). Similar to the St Petersburg ice slides, these roller coasters were positioned in pairs with the hills opposite each other, giving riders an opportunity for a convenient re-ride. The Belleville ride incorporated an important new feature that would change the engineering of roller coasters forever: locking the wheels to the track. Speeds approached an amazing 40 miles per hour. The

'Promenades Aeriennes' had two side-by-side tracks on its eighty-foot drop, making it the first 'racing' coaster. Upon reaching the bottom of the hill, the tracks split off to opposite sides and wrapped around the structure, coming back together at the station.

Below: The sun sets on Lake Shafer and the Hoosier Hurricane at Indiana Beach, Monticello, Indiana. A full specification of this 3000-foot long modern woodie can be found on page 41.

In the decades to come, several more gravity rides followed that were variations on the originals, until 1846, when an ingenious Paris engineer decided the time had come to add a vertical loop. The ride, consisting of a 30-foot high sloping track with a loop at the bottom, was built at Frascati Gardens. A single-rider car would travel 100 feet down the inclined track and catapult through the small loop, 13 feet in diameter. After the loop, the track sloped upward, and gravity would bring the tiny car to a stop.

Just about the time it seemed that everyone was enjoying these assorted amusement devices, the novelty wore off, and roller coasters and amusement parks in Europe virtually disappeared toward the end of the 19th century.

THE GRAVITY ROAD

Meanwhile, in the United States, another form of roller coaster was being developed in the coal-rich mountains of Mauch Chunk, Pennsylvania. In 1827, Josiah White, a mining company developer at Summit Hill, needed a way to transport tons of coal down the mountain. White developed a railway system known as the Gravity Road. Miners would fill cars with coal. Once loaded, the cars would be attached together in 'trains' of six to fourteen cars, and sent down the mountainside on the Gravity Road. One brave man would sit in the last car and, using a brake, ease the coal-filled cars down to their destination – a 30-minute trip. After unloading the coal at the bottom, mules were used to haul the cars back up to the mining area, a process that took some three hours.

It didn't take long for curious tourists to begin stopping by to watch the procedure and ask if they could take a scenic ride down the mountain. Soon, members of the general public could take a trip on the Gravity Road for just 50 cents. In 1845, White completed work on a return track, providing a complete circuit for the cars and eliminating the need for the tired mules. The cars were pushed back to the top of the mountain by a steam engine. Eventually, the 18-mile circuit became known as the Mauch Chunk Switchback Railway. By 1873, more than 35,000 tourists were enjoying the ride annually, and the now-popular area became known as the 'Switzerland of America.' The invention of the automobile and the depression of the early 1930s took their toll on the Mauch Chunk Switchback Railway, however, and the tourists

Right: Built by Philadelphia Toboggan Co., and a fixture at Canobie Lake Park, Salem, New Hampshire since 1936, this 2000-foot long woodie had been constructed at Lakewood Park, Connecticut six years earlier, but was purchased by the New England park and moved.

dwindled. In 1937, the Railway closed forever and the tracks were sold for scrap. Remnants of the famous tracks (which some regard as America's first railroad) still remain, and the Mauch Chunk Switchback Railway was named a historical monument in July 1976.

CONEY ISLAND

More roller coaster history was made in 1884 when an Indiana inventor named La Marcus Thompson designed a version of the switchback railway specifically for commercial use at amusement centers. Thompson debuted his invention on Tenth Avenue in Coney Island, Brooklyn, New York, and it became an instant success. The 600-foot long Switchback Railway at Coney Island cost five cents to ride and had a top speed of about six miles per hour. Cars were placed at the top of the 50-foot incline where they would travel by gravity down the hills, finally coming to rest at the top of a hill at the other end. Attendants would switch the car over to a parallel set of tracks and passengers would ride a mirror-image track back to the starting point. The ride was so popular that Thompson was able to recoup his $1600 investment in just three weeks. He patented his ride the following year.

Soon after Thompson's Switchback Railway began attracting crowds, another roller coaster opened at Coney Island. This one, the Serpentine Railway, built by Charles Alcoke, was notable because the track formed one continuous circuit, eliminating the need for the 'switchback' process. Passengers rode on seats resembling park benches facing to the sides of the ride rather than straight ahead. With these innocent beginnings, the amusement ride competition that would dominate Coney Island for decades had begun.

During the winter months of the late 1800s, large, well-built toboggan slides very similar to the Russian ice slides became popular in the United States. It was becoming obvious that America was eager to discover new ways to slide, roll, skate or float downhill. Boat chutes, all sizes of toboggan runs and an assortment of water slides became popular.

Californian Philip Hinkle entered the roller coaster race in 1885, and debuted the third Coney Island roller coaster. Hinkle's ride featured a taller hill and faster speeds than Thompson's or Alcoke's, and seats that faced forward. Soon, roller coasters began to appear in other locations across America, with increas-

Above: Dorney Park's Thunderhawk is a beautifully maintained Herbert Schmeck design dating from 1924. Its 2767-foot long, tree-lined course begins with an 80-foot lift.

ingly more creative configurations. Meanwhile, La Marcus Thompson was developing his idea of a form of ride where passengers could enjoy an imaginary scenic tour, and in 1887 opened the Scenic Railway in Atlantic City, New Jersey. Once again, Thompson had introduced the most popular amusement ride in the world. The ride was built over the sand, with one section indoors containing scenery, props and special effects. While riding through the indoor section of the Scenic Railway, passengers would travel past scenes from ancient times and elaborate painted landscapes accented with electric lights. Thompson formed the L. A. Thompson Scenic Railway Company in 1888, and began building

Right: In 1994 both Paramount's Kings Dominion (pictured), and Paramount's Carowinds commissioned a 3157-foot long woodie called the Hurler. International Coasters, Inc. built the identical rides, with theming based on the Wayne's World *movie.*

Left: Montezooma's Revenge, built for Knott's Berry Farm, Buena Park, California by Anton Schwarzkopf, is a shuttle loop coaster which reaches 55 miles per hour from a standstill in around three seconds. The train powers forward and backward through the station, the 76-foot loop, and up and down two steep inclines, in around thirty-five seconds.

the attractions across America, each one more detailed, panoramic and imaginative than the last. In 1910, his most elaborate Scenic Railway opened on a pier in Venice, California, completely themed throughout with artificial mountains and an Egyptian temple. Like Thompson's other Scenic Railways, this one was a tremendous success.

The 1893 World's Fair, known as the World's Columbian Exposition, held in Chicago, Illinois, marked another milestone in the development of amusement rides. The landmark attraction of the Fair was a massive 264-foot tall wheel that held more than 2,100 passengers at one time. It was engineered by George Ferris, who gave his name to the attraction.

In 1895, an Atlantic City lifeguard-turned-publicist named Paul Boyton brought his trained seal show to Coney Island and set up shop. The show was largely unsuccessful on its own, so Boyton decided to build a ride to stimulate business. A boat ramp was built that emptied into the same pool used for the seal show, and was named Shoot-the-Chutes – a ride that achieved immediate popularity. Boyton went on to add more rides (including a looping coaster called the Flip-Flap, designed by Lina Beecher) and the facility became known as Sea Lion Park, an establishment many consider to be America's first amusement park. Boyton is also credited for introducing the concept of an enclosed park with a gate admission.

Coney Island entrepreneur George Tilyou, who already owned a few rides scattered throughout Coney Island, watched Boyton's successful Sea Lion Park operation with its looping coaster and shoot-the-chutes. Tilyou began searching for a signature ride around which to build a park of his own. Capitalizing on the current popularity of horse racing, he constructed a 'Steeplechase' ride with a set of four parallel

Above: Greezed Lightnin', at AstroWorld, Houston, Texas, approaches the brakes and loading station at the end of a breathtaking ride. This coaster, and Montezooma's Revenge, left, were both built in 1978.

tracks that, instead of roller coaster cars, utilized mechanical horses. The horses would race along the thin rails powered by gravity. Tilyou added more rides and an elaborate entrance, and by 1897, Steeplechase Park was ready to compete with Boyton's Sea Lion Park.

The competition continued. Edwin Prescott debuted another looping roller coaster called the Loop-the-Loop at Coney Island in 1901. Cars carried only four passengers and circled the loop with nothing holding them onto the track but centrifugal force! Prescott is believed to be the first person ever to charge admission just to watch a ride. Although the ride was popular, it was not profitable, because of the low capacity. Another Loop-the-Loop coaster opened that same year in Atlantic City.

Sea Lion Park was bought out and expanded in 1903. And although the Flip-Flap looping

coaster was removed, the property soon became one of the most popular Coney Island amusement centers of all time: Luna Park.

The $3.5 million Dreamland, another spectacular park, opened one year later on Surf Avenue and featured a double shoot-the-chutes extending out into the Atlantic Ocean. The park became famous for its Swiss-themed Scenic Railway, Infant Incubator exhibit, and nightly show called Fighting Flames, where a six-story building was set on fire, then extinguished by firemen arriving on noisy, colorful fire engines.

Coney Island was attracting the curiosity of the world. Thousands of visitors at the amusement wonderland on a given summer afternoon in the early 1900s quickly became a million by 1915. Electric lights were being used by the

thousands. The hot dog was invented (and in some places they are still referred to as 'Coneys' or 'Coney Dogs' even today). America's first 'petting zoo' debuted, and in 1910, the first 'kiddieland' was introduced. But always in the middle of all the excitement: the roller coaster.

One of the most notorious of the early Coney Island thrill machines was Drop-the-Dips, which opened in June 1907. The brainchild of Christopher Feucht, this 60-foot high roller coaster was the first built to be intentionally severe. Soon, newspapers began to write about the intensity of the ride, and Feucht watched as attendance increased as a result. Drop-the-Dips burned to the ground in July 1907 – just a month after it opened. Feucht immediately built a new one, even more ferocious than the origi-

Above: Orient Express, an Arrow-built looper built in 1980 at Worlds Of Fun, Kansas City, Missouri, features a first drop of 115 feet at 55 degrees, and interlocking loops (pictured) in a 3470-foot woodland layout.

nal, and its popularity was sustained. In addition to being considered the first high speed roller coaster, it also was the first to utilize a lap bar to secure riders in their seats.

Throughout the next decade, thanks in part to the unparalleled success of Coney Island, amusement parks were being built all over the world, but they were the most popular in the United States. During this time, it is estimated that somewhere between 1500 to 2000 roller coasters dotted the countryside. Dozens of new rides with unusual names like the Tickler, Dip-Lo-Docus, Mystic Screw, Virginia Reel, Cyclone Bowl and Hooper-Reverser were invented. Scenic Railways, Figure-eights, racing coasters,

Below: The 1980 thriller Orient Express (left) featured the world's first boomerang element, a twist since adopted by many other steel coasters, including Goudurix, which was built in 1989 at Parc Asterix, north of Paris, France.

Steeplechase rides; roller coasters of all shapes and sizes were being built just about everywhere.

One of the figure-eight style coasters built during this era (1902) was Leap-the-Dips in Altoona, Pennsylvania. Designed by E. Joy Morris, this 'side-friction' coaster (the individual cars had wheels positioned perpendicular to the running wheels that ran along wooden rails on the edges of the track) has survived through

the years and remains at Altoona's Lakemont Park. Standing but not operating at the time of this publication, Leap-the-Dips is the oldest existing roller coaster and the last example of the classic figure-eight design in the world. Fund-raising efforts are well underway to renovate this historic ride, with hopes that it can operate again before the turn of the century.

During this coaster-building boom of the early 1900s, La Marcus Thompson's chief engi-

neer, John Miller, was busy designing rides and securing patents for dozens of vital roller coaster components like the ratchets that keep the cars from rolling back down the lift hill, the underwheels that lock the cars to the track, brakes, and others. In addition to Thompson, he worked with several other coaster builders, and in 1911, began designing coasters for the Philadelphia Toboggan Company.

In 1920, John Miller teamed up with another coaster builder, Harry Baker, and their resulting company was responsible for more than 50 roller coasters until the two dissolved their firm and went their separate ways in 1923. Both continued producing rides on their own. While Baker went on to build a few more coasters, including the Coney Island Cyclone, which opened in 1927, Miller formed the John A. Miller Co. in Illinois, and continued to design and construct roller coasters by the dozens, including the Coney Island Thunderbolt, which also opened in 1927.

As the Great Depression swept America in 1929 and into the 1930s, the 'Golden Age of Roller Coasters' came to an abrupt end. But Miller was a survivor, and this time decided to team up with World War I pilot Norman Bartlett. Soon, the two began marketing a new type of roller coaster called the Flying Turns. The Flying Turns was a bobsled-type ride in which the cars rode freely in a wooden trough with high-banked sides, rather than being attached to a track. A few Flying Turns were built, the most famous of which was installed at Euclid Beach Park in Cleveland, Ohio in 1930. With the state of the economy, however, Bartlett and Miller were unable to stay in business and parted company in 1932.

In addition to his many influences, accomplishments, patents and inventions (many of which are commonly used in roller coaster design today), Miller was the first designer to break the 100-foot tall coaster plateau. He died in 1941, and is remembered as possibly the single most influential force in American roller coaster history. A few of the master builder's coasters still remain, to be enjoyed by today's generation of thrill seekers: they include all three wooden coasters at Kennywood Park near Pittsburgh, Pennsylvania (the Thunderbolt was built from Miller's original Pippin coaster); and wooden coasters at Clementon Park, Clementon, New Jersey; Geauga Lake, Aurora, Ohio; and Blackpool Pleasure Beach in England.

The Golden Age of Roller Coasters was also dominated by dynamic rides built by legendary designers like Harry Traver, Frederick Church, Arthur Looff, Fred Pearce, Edward Vettel and Herbert Schmeck.

Some of the most terrifying wooden coasters ever built came from the Traver Engineering

Company, under the direction of Harry Traver. Remembered in amusement circles for his legendary coasters, Traver also gave us less violent classics like the Tumble Bug, Laff in the Dark and Circle Swing rides. His roller coaster designs include the first coaster ever to be named 'Cyclone,' the coaster for the 1926 Sesquicentennial Exposition, in Philadelphia.

But Traver saved his most outrageous introductions for the following year. In 1927, Traver unleashed the most fearsome lineup of coasters yet, including extreme thrillers like the radical

Above: The structure of Atlanta's Georgia Cyclone begins to take shape. This Curtis D Summers design was squeezed into a compact, three-acre site, echoing the steep drops and tight turns of Coney Island's Cyclone.
See page 54 for views of the completed coaster.

Revere Beach Lightning in Massachusetts, the Oaks Park Zip in Oregon, and possibly the most intense wooden roller coaster ever built: the Crystal Beach Cyclone near Niagara Falls, Ontario, Canada.

The most infamous ride ever built at Revere Beach, the Lightning gained an instant reputation for fear when a woman reportedly became hysterical during a ride and jumped to her death on the second night of its operation. During the ride's short six-year life span, injuries were common. Large crowds would gather to watch, but few would be brave enough to ride, and the unprofitable Lightning was dismantled in 1933; it was just too wild for the general public.

The Oaks Park Zip was cut back severely from its planned length of 3200 feet to 2500

Below: Spectacular blossoms provide the backdrop for the rocketing Bandit, at Yomiuri Land in Tokyo. Built by TOGO Japan in 1988, the fastest stretches of the ride produce speeds approaching 70 miles per hour.

feet, resulting in a tight, spiraling, convoluted layout. The rough track included a first drop angled at 80 degrees. Like the Lightning, injuries were common, especially to the arms and ribs, and it, too, was torn down due to lack of ridership just seven years after its debut.

White knuckle thrill seekers met their match when the Crystal Beach Cyclone invaded the Lake Erie shoreline in 1927. With a ride time of only 40 seconds, the 3,000-foot long Cyclone was so twisted that there was no level place anywhere on the entire tracks to put brakes except in the loading station. It gained notoriety as the only coaster in history to have a full-time nurse on duty in the station. When it was demolished in 1946, parts of the Cyclone's structure were used to build the Crystal Beach Comet, which continues to operate today at The Great Escape

park in Lake George, New York (page 75).

Designer Frederick Church teamed with business partner Thomas Prior and worked with Harry Traver on several coasters in the mid-to-late 1920s. Prior & Church are remembered mainly for their 'Bobs'-style coasters and the legendary Aero Coaster designed by Church and built at Playland, Rye, New York in 1928, an engineering masterpiece regarded by many as the most elegantly designed roller coaster in history, with its great combination of speed and thrills. The last surviving Prior & Church ride still operates at Mission Beach, San Diego, California (the Giant Dipper – page 32).

California's other beautiful Giant Dipper (located on the Santa Cruz Beach Boardwalk – page 31), is a tribute to the design work of Arthur Looff, whose father, Charles, was a noted

carousel designer and carver. Father and son Looff worked together on a variety of amusement rides, including coasters, and originally opened the Santa Monica Pier in Southern California – which continues to entertain guests today with a historic carousel, a steel roller coaster and other attractions at Pacific Park.

Below: The Sidewinder, at Hersheypark, Hershey, Pennsylvania, is a Vekoma International design with a compact footprint which allows installation in a small area – a major advantage for many parks.

Fred Pearce and his family were responsible for building thirty roller coasters and several complete amusement parks between 1905 and 1929. Coasters to their credit include the massive 90-foot tall Trip Thru the Clouds at Riverview Park, Detroit, Michigan. Built in 1915, the track measured more than a mile long. Fred's contributions to the amusement business include the first use of pressure-treated lumber in construction, greatly extending the lives of roller coaster structures.

Edward Vettel and his nephew Andy were influential in designing some thrilling coasters

that are still in existence today. Ed's classic Cyclone still thrills riders at Lakeside Park in Denver, Colorado, and his Blue Streak at Conneaut Lake Park, Pennsylvania, although currently closed, contains three drops that produce some of the most intense negative Gs of any coaster in the world. Andy Vettel is best known for redesigning the Kennywood Thunderbolt in 1968, utilizing existing first and last drops of John Miller's 1924 Pippin.

The Philadelphia Toboggan Company opened in 1904 and is still doing business today, using the name Philadelphia Toboggan Coasters, Inc.

During its long, colorful history, the company has been responsible for building more than 70 carousels, approximately 150 roller coasters, and hundreds of roller coaster cars. During the Golden Age, several noted coaster designers worked for the firm, including Herbert Schmeck, designer of dozens of rides between 1917 and 1955. Many of Schmeck's excellent creations are still in use today. His projects included working with John Miller on the Paragon Park Giant Coaster in 1917 (now the Wild One at Adventure World, Largo, Maryland – page 63); the Rocket at Playland Park, San Antonio in 1947, which was moved to Knoebels Amusement Resort in Pennsylvania and renamed the Phoenix in 1985 (page 71); and in 1947, the Comet at Crystal Beach Park, relocated to The Great Escape,

Lake George, New York (page 75) in 1994.

John Allen became president of PTC in 1954 and principal designer for the firm, picking up where Schmeck left off. Allen designed more than 20 coasters, including long-running greats like the Swamp Fox in Myrtle Beach, South Carolina in 1966; the Cannonball at Lake Winnepesaukah, Rossville, Georgia in 1967; the Great American Scream Machine at Six Flags Over Georgia in 1973 and the Screamin' Eagle at Six Flags Over Mid America which opened in 1976 (page 39).

Under the guidance of president Tom Rebbie, Philadelphia Toboggan Coasters thrives today by providing roller coaster cars for other coaster builders, along with other key components like fin braking systems, queue line gates, and coaster

Above: Le Boomerang, at La Ronde, Montreal, Canada, is an identical ride to Sidewinder, (facing page), except for the paint job. The coaster produces a total of six inversions.

car replacement parts. Offering two-seater, three-seater, junior-size and 'California-style' (fiberglass body) cars, PTC has become the vehicle supplier for nearly every wooden roller coaster installation worldwide.

During the relatively 'quiet' coaster-building years following the Depression, one of the few competitors that the Philadelphia Toboggan Company had was Ohio-based National Amusement Device (NAD). Although they built only a few roller coasters, their trademark stainless steel trains (some featuring headlights on

the front car) remain art deco treasures. NAD cars can still be enjoyed on both Camden Park's Big Dipper and Lil' Dipper in Huntington, West Virginia; the Kennywood Thunderbolt (page 68); the Serpent of Fire in Mexico City (page 78) and a few others. Sadly, the historic cars have all but disappeared elsewhere.

THE DISNEY EFFECT

Changing times in the 1950s and 1960s spelled the end for many traditional amusement parks and the roller coasters in them. In 1955, Walt Disney opened Disneyland in Southern California, and suddenly, the 'theme park' idea was the new buzz in the amusement industry. (While Walt's park is a masterpiece, many other parks argue that his was not the first 'theme park.' Themed parks in existence before Disneyland include Indiana's Holiday World, New York's Great Escape and California's Knott's Berry Farm, all of which claim the title). A new era in amusement parks was dawning, a new group of roller coaster designers was on the horizon, and modern steel coasters were about to make their grand entrance.

Disneyland's Matterhorn Bobsleds roller coaster. which opened for the first time in 1959, was very significant for several reasons. It was

the first to utilize tubular steel rails – an innovation in engineering and construction that became the basis for an entire industry's new roller coaster technology. (Coasters that ran on metal tracks were nothing new, but previous – and portable – rides like the Wild Mouse and Galaxy coasters did not use tubular steel track). The Matterhorn was engineered and manufactured by the Arrow Development Company of Mountain View, California, and its vehicles ran on quiet nylon-covered steel wheels. In all, Arrow designed transportation systems for several attractions at Disneyland, including Mr Toad's Wild Ride, the Mad Hatter's Tea Party, two trains and two dark rides. Arrow also refurbished the park's carousel. Even the tram that brings guests in from the parking lot to Disneyland's front gate was built by Arrow.

As Six Flags, Busch and Kings Entertainment theme parks were developed in the 1960s and 1970s, Arrow was called upon to provide some of the larger rides. Karl Bacon, one of Arrow's three founders, developed a flume ride in 1963, a runaway mine ride in 1966, and began developing ideas for a corkscrew roller coaster in 1968. Arrow quickly became the front-running competitor in the steel coaster 'arms race.' Arrow turned the amusement industry upside-

Above: Big Bad Wolf, at Busch Gardens Williamsburg, Williamsburg, Virginia, was the third suspended coaster produced by Arrow Dynamics, following the Bat and XLR-8. Built in 1984, the 2800-foot long ride employs two lifts, from the second of which the cars plunge 99 feet towards the 'Rhine River,' swinging left at the last minute to avoid the water.

down with the introduction of the corkscrew roller coaster at Knott's Berry Farm in 1975 (currently operating at Silverwood Theme Park in Athol, Idaho). In the early 1980s, Arrow introduced another innovation, the suspended coaster. With coaches hanging from an overhead track, the suspended coaster gives riders the feeling of free flight as it swings out at banked curves and soars through the air. To date, Arrow has manufactured ten suspended coasters throughout the world, nine of which are still in operation, including Vortex at Paramount Canada's Wonderland (page 82).

Arrow re-introduced the classic shoot-the-chutes boat ride to the industry at the 1984 New Orleans World's Fair. The ride sent 20-passenger boats plummeting down its 60-foot drop into a splash pond below, creating a rebirth in the classic ride. Arrow Dynamics continues to build steel roller coasters, ranging from record-setting non-looping hypercoasters like the Desperado at Buffalo Bill's Resort Casino (page 34) and The Pepsi Max Big One at Blackpool Pleasure Beach (page 88), to intense, multi-inversion thrillers like Six Flags Magic Mountain's Viper (page 28) and the Drachen Fire at Busch Gardens Williamsburg (page 66).

RETURN OF THE LOOP

In 1975, Switzerland's Intamin AG in conjunction with Germany's Schwarzkopf Inc. was credited with building the first loop coaster since the early wooden versions built at the turn of the century. The firm built the Revolution coaster at Six Flags Magic Mountain, and soon after manufactured similar rides for Hersheypark (the SooperDooperLooper) and Six Flags Over Georgia (Mind Bender). Intamin/Schwarzkopf also pioneered the shuttle loop coaster in 1976 with the installation of King Kobra at Kings Dominion in Doswell, Virginia. The shuttle loop is designed to catapult a train from a standing start out of the station and down a straight section of track, through a vertical loop, and up a 138-foot tall ramp (Montezooma's Revenge and Greezed Lightnin' are examples). When the train loses momentum on the ramp, it stops and repeats the process backward, through the loop and through the station, backing up onto a reverse ramp, losing momentum again and gliding into the station brakes.

Intamin and Schwarzkopf eventually split into separate companies, and both have continued to supply the world with exciting roller coasters. Schwarzkopf's amazing inventions include the indoor triple-looping Mindbender at West Edmonton Mall (page 81), and larger versions like the portable four-loop Thriller and five-loop Olympia Looping Bahn coasters that can be enjoyed at German fairs each summer.

Intamin's creations have been equally unique, and include rides like the Space Diver (called Flashback at Six Flags Magic Mountain); Freefall (see page 99); Bobsled rides like the indoor Disaster Transport at Cedar Point and the outdoor Screamin' Delta Demon at Nashville, Tennessee's Opryland; and standing coasters like Batman the Escape at Six

Above and below: The Vampire, at Chessington World Of Adventures, Chessington, Surrey, England, is a 2220-foot suspended coaster designed in 1990 by Arrow Dynamics for the park's 'Transylvania' themed area. Boarding through castle ruins, riders simulate the flight of a vampire bat, darting over the rooftops and swooping into an underground tunnel.

Above: West Edmonton Mall, in Edmonton, Alberta, Canada, houses the only indoor triple-looping coaster in the world, the amazing Mindbender. It's an intense ride in every respect, particularly through the tight, fast third loop, where riders pull over five Gs.

Flags AstroWorld in Houston, Texas. Intamin is one of two firms debuting coasters powered by linear induction motors in 1996. Superman the Escape at Six Flags Magic Mountain illustrates another major technological advance for roller coasters. The ride is expected to shatter existing speed (more than 100 miles per hour) and height records (415 feet) for roller coasters and thrill rides in general.

When Angus Wynne Jr. prepared to build the nation's first regional theme park – Six Flags Over Texas – in 1961, he asked local civil engineer William Cobb if he would accept a position as structural engineer for the park. Cobb thought it sounded like an interesting job, and was introduced to the world of amusement rides. Cobb eventually became involved in the design and construction of 11 new roller coasters and two remodeling projects (a total of six coasters for the Six Flags Theme Parks). Cobb worked closely with PTC's John Allen on the construction of the Great American Scream Machine at Six Flags Over Georgia in 1972, and the Screamin' Eagle at Six Flags Over Mid-America the following year. Winner of the President's award for a 'lifetime of outstanding contributions to the amusement industry' from the International Association of Amusement Parks and Attractions in 1987, Cobb is probably best remembered for applying his design talents to the Texas Cyclone at Six Flags AstroWorld; the Riverside Cyclone (page 72) and the dual-tracked Le Monstre at La Ronde (page 84). Unfortunately, he never got the chance to see his design for the wicked Texas Giant coaster come to reality. Cobb died in 1990, leaving us with some of the most notable coasters in the United States, Canada and France.

For 18 years, Cobb's partner was John Pierce, a design engineer who worked in the same office. Pierce assisted in the designs of Cobb's coasters, and continued the tradition of engineering excellence in wooden coasters after Cobb's death. Pierce was involved in the moving and reconstruction of Kansas City's Fairyland Wildcat to Frontier City in Oklahoma, work on reprofiling of the Wild One and Hercules, and the designs of the Rattler, White Canyon, and Twister II, before his retirement from coaster designing in 1995.

In 1953, the TOGO corporation, based in Japan, produced that country's first major roller coaster at Asakusa Hanayashiki park in Tokyo. This remains the oldest operating coaster in Japan. Twenty-two years later, TOGO introduced Asia's largest roller coaster, and, in 1979, TOGO's first loop coaster was installed in Japan. Two years later, TOGO further developed the inversion coaster by adding a corkscrew element and the first 'Loop and Screw Coaster' was built, entirely over a lake. TOGO continued to introduce new attractions to Japan's amusement industry, and in 1980, built what was, at the time, the world's largest Giant Wheel, a continually revolving marvel 203 feet in diameter.

STANDING ROOM ONLY

In 1982, the Standing Coaster made its world debut and in 1984, TOGO exported the ride to the United States (Kings Island). Named the King Cobra, the ride gave roller coasters a thrilling new dimension. In the mid-1980s, similar TOGO standing coasters were installed at Kings Dominion and Canada's Wonderland (page 83). In 1986, the firm's unusual Ultra Twister coaster was exported to the United States and installed at Six Flags Great Adventure in Jackson, New Jersey. It operates today at Six Flags AstroWorld.

One of the world's fastest coasters, with a height difference of 256 feet was built in 1988 by TOGO at Japan's Yomiuri Land park. A sprawling, non-looping hyper-coaster, the 5117-foot long Bandit (page 94) attains speeds of 69 miles per hour. TOGO and Namco joined forces to bring Zola, the world's first interactive laser roller coaster to Fujiku Highland park that same year. In 1991, TOGO completed work on an indoor amusement park in Northern Japan called the Tomakomai Fantasy Dome. Among the 20 major attractions housed in this complex is a 114-foot high, 2443-foot long TOGO Super Roller Coaster which reaches speeds of 66 miles per hour.

At the 1992 amusement industry trade show, TOGO received awards in the New Technology and New Ride categories for their Mega Coaster. The Mega Coaster is capable of record heights, speeds of 80 miles per hour, multiple inversions and 360-degree 'heartline' rolls. The world's first Mega Coaster, (the Viper) was installed at Six Flags Great Adventure in 1975 on the exact site previously occupied by the Ultra Twister. America's tallest Mega Coaster (the 203-foot tall Big Apple) will open in late 1996 at the New York New York casino-entertainment complex in Las Vegas, Nevada. A record-breaking 257-foot tall coaster utilizing Mega Coaster technology will also open in 1996 at Japan's Fujikyu Highland park.

O.D. Hopkins and Associates, most noted for their water attractions like log flumes, shoot-the-chutes and river rapids rides, have also contributed some exciting additions to the roller coaster scene in the United States. Beginning with the 80-foot tall double-looping Texas

Right: The Viper, designed and built by Arrow Dynamics in 1990 at Six Flags Magic Mountain, Valencia, California, peaks at 188 feet and is North America's tallest looping coaster. *See page 29 for Viper's specification.*

Tornado at Wonderland Park in Amarillo, Hopkins has gone on to manufacture five more coasters including the Red Devil at Ghost Town in the Sky, Maggie Valley, North Carolina, which provides riders with possibly the most spectacular mountain view of any coaster in the world; and two rides at Castles & Coasters in Phoenix, Arizona.

FROM THE NETHERLANDS TO THE WORLD

Record sales and innovative new rides have highlighted the past decade for Vekoma International, a ride manufacturer based in the Netherlands offering a wide range of amusement products and roller coasters. During the last 15 years, the company's most popular roller coaster has been the exciting Boomerang, a unique compact coaster which turns riders upside-down six times (three forward and three backward) during its two-minute journey. Vekoma has installed 25 of the rides in parks worldwide. In 1996, the company will debut its first Inverted Boomerang called the Invertigo. The ride has the same track configuration as the standard Boomerang, but the cars are suspended from the track overhead.

Sweden's Liseburg park will open the prototype – named the Hangover – in 1996.

Another of Vekoma's successful innovations has been the Suspended Looping Coaster, a ride which sends passengers through a variety of inverted elements seated two-across in ski-lift style chairs suspended from twisting tracks above. Dubbed the Condor, the suspended looping coaster made its world debut in 1994 at Walibi Flevo in the Netherlands. Five North American parks quickly ordered similar rides for the 1996 season, including Morey's Pier in Wildwood, New Jersey, which situated their unit within a maze of water attractions and other rides, adding to the drama of the ride experience. The Great Nor'Easter (page 76) proved to be an unparalleled success at the popular summertime playground. So far, nearly a dozen of the Vekoma thrillers have been installed worldwide, including Lethal Weapon – The Ride at Warner Brothers Movie World in Australia, and the suspended looping coaster is shaping up to be the firm's newest hit.

In addition to the thrilling 'standard' models, Vekoma has also been very successful with their custom designs around the world, most notably in France with Space Mountain (page 86) and Big Thunder Mountain at Disneyland Paris and the seven-inversion Goudurix at Parc Asterix (page 85).

The Italian S&MC company, represented in the United States by Premier Rides, is a custom ride builder which also offers a catalog of standard steel coasters. Their most popular to date has been the Hurricane, a modern version of the compact Galaxy coaster. Hurricanes can be found in several parks, including Santa Cruz Beach Boardwalk in California, Playland and Adventureland in New York, and a themed indoor installation at Six Flags Over Texas. S&MC also manufactured the High Roller – a relatively small steel coaster but custom-designed to be placed atop the Stratosphere Tower in Las Vegas. Upon its debut in 1996, the

Below: Another woodie takes shape. This Wildcat has a home at Hersheypark, Hershey, Pennsylvania. It is seen under construction in 1995, when track laying had begun on the completed structural sections.

High Roller will become the highest roller coaster in the world by far, operating at more than 900 feet in the air.

In addition to the High Roller and Texas Hurricane ride, S&MC will simultaneously introduce two technologically advanced coasters at Paramount's Kings Island and Kings Dominion parks in 1996. The identical Outer Limits – Flight of Fear coasters will launch passengers using a linear induction motor system into a contorted track configuration concealed by darkness in an enclosed structure, highlighted

Above: Bolliger & Mabillard's inverted coaster for Busch Gardens Tampa Bay, pictured here as an artist's rendition, features a 128-foot dive into an excavated trench at 65 miles per hour. Located in the Egypt-themed section of the park, Montu, named for an ancient Egyptian Sun God, turns riders upside down seven times over 3983 feet of track, and features a 104-foot tall vertical loop.
Right: This photograph, taken in 1995, shows the lower sections of Montu's lift hill being positioned.

with themed sound and lighting effects. After negotiating the looping track, the train will stop to let riders exit, and will return to the original loading station empty, giving oncoming passengers the eerie feeling that no one is coming out.

TALL TIMBER MEN

From the mid-1980s through the early 1990s, the wooden coaster scene was dominated by the design and construction teams of Curtis D Summers and Charles Dinn. Dinn was construction manager for the Beast at Kings Island in 1979, and was called upon to supervise the 1985 relocation of the San Antonio Rocket to Knoebel's Amusement Resort. The Rocket relocation sparked an interest in relocating abandoned wooden coasters to other parks, and soon Dinn was busy moving the Giant Coaster from Paragon Park to Wild World, and the Skyliner from Roseland Park to Lakemont Park.

With the renewed interest in wooden coasters, other parks decided to add new rides, so a collaboration began with Ohio structural engi-

Below: Cedar Point, Ohio's twelfth coaster project is Mantis, a 145-foot tall stand-up monster featuring a dive loop and an inclined loop, neither of which have been previously used on a stand-up ride. It is also the fastest ride of its kind, reaching a speed of 60 miles per hour at the base of the 137-foot first drop.

neer Summers, and builder Dinn. Although Summers' firm was responsible for designing a total of 32 coasters, it was those with Dinn that he will most be remembered for.

Exciting thrillers like the Timber Wolf, Texas Giant, Hercules and Mean Streak were products of their teamwork. Summers' last design was a team effort with Intamin, producing the Pegasus at Efteling park in the Netherlands. Summers died of a heart attack in 1992, exactly one year to the day after the opening of his biggest project, Cedar Point's Mean Streak.

During the relocation of the Phoenix, Dinn's daughter Denise helped out at the construction site. After working with her father on forthcoming coaster projects, Denise Dinn soon learned the business and, following her father's retirement in 1991, formed her own company to continue the family tradition of building wooden roller coasters. In 1992, her company, Custom Coasters Inc. (now known as Custom Coasters International), built its first ride – the family oriented Sky Princess at Dutch Wonderland in Lancaster, Pennsylvania. Since that time, the company has flourished and now has nearly a dozen projects under its belt, including its first international roller coaster, the Mega Fobia at Oakwood leisure park in Wales. CCI designers Larry Bill and Dennis McNulty represent forerunners of the new generation of wooden roller coaster engineers.

The Swiss firm of Bolliger & Mabillard (named for principal engineers Walter Bolliger and Claude Mabillard), took the amusement industry by storm when they appeared on the

scene in 1990, introducing the Iron Wolf standing coaster at Six Flags Great America near Gurnee, Illinois. Since that debut, B&M has been among the most sought-after amusement ride manufacturers in modern history. The innovative concepts, technological superiority and flawless construction of their coasters have had theme parks around the world scrambling to get in line to order their new generation creations. The firm's biggest innovation to date, B&M introduced the inverted coaster in 1992 by delivering Batman the Ride to an eager audience at Six Flags Great America. The reaction was so positive that Six Flags Theme Parks ordered Batman inverted coasters for three more parks for the 1993, 1994 and 1995 seasons. Larger B&M inverted coasters have been installed at Cedar Point (Raptor – page 52), and the largest yet, Busch Gardens Tampa Bay (Montu). B&M's inverted creations feature breathtaking heartline spins and outside-looping elements never previously attempted on roller coasters.

In addition to their inverted coasters, B&M has also revolutionized sitting and standing coasters. Four-across seating and record-breaking new elements highlight multi-inversion thrillers like Kumba at Busch Gardens Tampa Bay and the eight-inversion Dragon Khan at Port Aventura in Spain (page 92). B&M's design creativity and attention to detail are also displayed in their standing coasters, the largest of which is the 145-foot tall Mantis, new for 1996 at Cedar Point.

Based in La Selva Beach, California and founded in 1983, Morgan Manufacturing – a

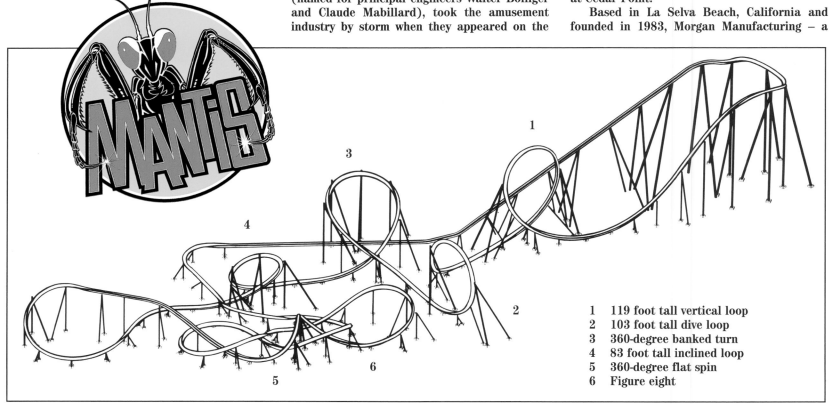

1	119 foot tall vertical loop
2	103 foot tall dive loop
3	360-degree banked turn
4	83 foot tall inclined loop
5	360-degree flat spin
6	Figure eight

Left: The 1149-foot tall Stratosphere Tower, seen under construction in the summer of 1995, is the tallest free-standing tower in the United States, and features the highest coaster ever built – the High Roller – which wraps itself around the tower at the 909-foot plateau. Above: A section of the bright red track is winched into position using the tower crane.

multi-faceted ride manufacturing company – came to be known in the roller coaster industry for supplying fiberglass-body cars built for new and existing wooden coasters. In 1994, that segment of the business was sold to Philadelphia Toboggan Coasters, Inc., enabling the company to turn its full attention to designing and manufacturing rides. The first two Morgan-built steel coasters will make their debut in 1996, with the 200-foot tall non-looping Wild Thing at Valleyfair! in Shakopee, Minnesota and the WestCoaster at Pacific Pier in Santa Monica, California. Morgan is also producing a mine adventure coaster for the Hecker Pass theme park, currently on the drawing boards for Gilroy, California.

Great Coasters International was formed in 1995, combining the roller coaster design and engineering talents of Michael Boodley with the construction expertise of Clair Hain. The company's first major project was the design and construction of the Wildcat roller coaster at Hersheypark, for the 1996 season.

As amusement ride technology speeds into the 21st century, thrill seekers can only dream of what is to come. Records for height, length and speed continue to be broken with each new season. Incredibly, roller coasters leave this century the same way they came in: the most popular attraction in the park.

Chapter Two

THE COASTER FILE

We all have our favorites;
we may prefer wood, or steel;
most of us could add to the list.
One thing, however, is certain.
The entries here represent
over fifty of the very best
roller coaster rides
in the world today.

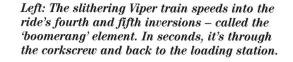

Left: The slithering Viper train speeds into the ride's fourth and fifth inversions – called the 'boomerang' element. In seconds, it's through the corkscrew and back to the loading station.

Below: Up to 28 passengers can experience the twisted excitement of Viper. The tallest complete-circuit looping coaster in North America turns riders upside-down seven times.

LOCATION: Six Flags Magic Mountain, Valencia, California, USA
YEAR BUILT: 1990
CONSTRUCTOR: Arrow Dynamics
MAXIMUM HEIGHT: 188 feet
LENGTH: 3830 feet
TOP SPEED: 70 mph
CAPACITY PER TRAIN: 28
LONGEST DROP: 171 feet
RIDE DURATION: 2 minutes 30 seconds
INVERSIONS: 7

The third and largest in a series of seven-inversion steel roller coasters built by Arrow Dynamics for Six Flags parks (similar, smaller versions were introduced at Chicago's Great America in 1988 and New Jersey's Great Adventure in 1989), the $8 million Viper reigns as the tallest multi-element coaster of its kind in North America.

The coiled structure, built in 1990, includes sixteen changes in elevation and – following a 17-story first drop, – features three vertical loops, topping out in order at 140 feet, 90 feet and 62 feet; followed by a disorienting boomerang element and corkscrew before returning exhilarated passengers back to the loading station.

Left: Although the 188-foot tall Viper is the tallest of the three Six Flags multi-loopers, it's not half as tall as Magic Mountain's 385-foot hexagonal Sky Tower, which was built by Intamin AG in 1971, the year the park opened to the public.

BOOMERANG

LOCATION: Knott's Berry Farm, Buena Park,
 California, USA
YEAR BUILT: 1990
CONSTRUCTOR: Vekoma International
MAXIMUM HEIGHT: 125 feet
LENGTH: 875 feet
TOP SPEED: 48 mph
CAPACITY PER TRAIN: 28
LONGEST DROP: 125 feet
RIDE DURATION: 1 minute 54 seconds
INVERSIONS: 6 (3 forward, 3 backward)

*Above: Boomerang is identical to more than
two dozen Boomerang coasters internationally,
making it the world's most popular major
production steel coaster to date.*

Since 1982, the Boomerang's compact structure
and design have helped make it a favorite of
parks everywhere. By 1996, 25 identical
Boomerang coasters were operating internationally, the Knott's unit being number 17.
    The train is pulled backward up a 125-foot
incline, then released to travel back through the
station, through the boomerang element and the
vertical loop and up an incline similar to the
first. Seconds later, gravity takes over and the
process is repeated in reverse.

*Right: Riders are turned upside-down a total
of six times during the two-minute Boomerang
ride at Knott's Berry Farm.*

GIANT DIPPER

LOCATION: Santa Cruz Beach Boardwalk,
  Santa Cruz, California, USA
YEAR BUILT: 1924
CONSTRUCTOR: Arthur Looff
MAXIMUM HEIGHT: 70 feet
LENGTH: 2640 feet
TOP SPEED: 55 mph
CAPACITY PER TRAIN: 24
LONGEST DROP: 65 feet
RIDE DURATION: 1 minute 52 seconds
INVERSIONS: 0

Santa Cruz resident Arthur Looff (son of famed carousel horse carver Charles Looff) envisioned a giant seaside wooden coaster that would be a "combination earthquake, balloon ascension and aeroplane drop." In 1924 that dream became a reality. Built in just 49 days, the coaster remains the most popular ride on the boardwalk today. Its 65-foot drop and sweeping fan turns have thrilled more than 40 million riders in person, and countless more by virtue of its many appearances in commercials and feature films.

Bottom: The classic Giant Dipper was built at a cost of $50,000. Today, it costs over $200,000 for the materials and labor just to paint it!

Below, inset: Seen from the skyway gondolas, the Giant Dipper was designated as a National Historic Landmark by the US National Park Service in June, 1987.

GIANT DIPPER

LOCATION: Belmont Park, Mission Beach,
 San Diego, California, USA
YEAR BUILT: 1925
CONSTRUCTOR: Prior & Church
MAXIMUM HEIGHT: 70 feet
LENGTH: 2600 feet
TOP SPEED: 45 mph
CAPACITY PER TRAIN: 24
LONGEST DROP: 60 feet
RIDE DURATION: 1 minute 55 seconds
INVERSIONS: 0

A classic example of the engineering skills of master coaster builders Prior and Church, the twisting Belmont Park Giant Dipper originally opened in 1925. Highlighted by a swooping first drop and series of hairpin turns, the curvy ride entertained millions for decades, just a block from the Pacific Ocean. Sadly, however, the park and the ride closed in 1976, and the Dipper fell into disrepair. But thanks to the preservation efforts of the Save The Coaster Committee, the public's attention was captured and the vintage ride was declared a National Historic Landmark, saving it from imminent demolition. In 1990 it was extensively renovated, outfitted with new trains, and reopened to the public.

Right: Built in 1925 by the respected coaster building team of Prior & Church, the twisting Belmont Park Giant Dipper features 2600 feet of graceful hills and exciting curves.

CANYON BLASTER

Only in Las Vegas will you find a double-looping pink roller coaster zooming around inside a 300,000 square foot glass dome. Despite (or maybe thanks to) its relatively small quarters, the Canyon Blaster packs quite a punch. After the loops, the 28-passenger train flips through a corkscrew, finishing with a 360-degree upward spiral and a wide right turn around the base of the canyon back to the station. The ride serves as the centerpiece of a five-acre themed 'adventuredome' caled Grand Slam Canyon, attached to the Circus Circus casino/entertainment complex.

LOCATION: Grand Slam Canyon at Circus Circus, Las Vegas, Nevada, USA
YEAR BUILT: 1993
CONSTRUCTOR: Arrow Dynamics
MAXIMUM HEIGHT: 94 feet
LENGTH: 2423 feet
TOP SPEED: 55 mph
CAPACITY PER TRAIN: 28
LONGEST DROP: 76 feet
RIDE DURATION: 1 minute 45 seconds
INVERSIONS: 4

Below: Pink steel track and rock formations highlight a ride on Las Vegas' Canyon Blaster, where an exciting ride is never a gamble.

Below: Animated prehistoric animals look on as riders scream through the elements of this indoor double-looper at Grand Slam Canyon.

DESPERADO

LOCATION: Buffalo Bill's Resort Casino,
   Stateline, Nevada, USA
YEAR BUILT: 1994
CONSTRUCTOR: Arrow Dynamics
MAXIMUM HEIGHT: 209 feet
LENGTH: 5843 feet
TOP SPEED: 80 mph
CAPACITY PER TRAIN: 30
LONGEST DROP: 225 feet
RIDE DURATION: 2 minutes 43 seconds
INVERSIONS: 0

Arrow designers literally went through the roof when they teamed up with Primadonna Resorts to create the tallest continuous-circuit roller coaster in North America: Desperado. Located in and wrapped around Buffalo Bill's Resort Casino complex on the California/Nevada border, this 209-foot tall looping speedster burns up the desert at close to 80 miles per hour. The ride begins inside the casino building, exiting through the roof. After a record-tying 225-foot drop into a tunnel, Desperado rockets skyward into a left-banking 155-foot swoop curve, a 360-degree spiral, three air-time-filled rabbit hops, and eventually into a twisting dive through a manmade stone formation. Finishing the dizzying journey covering nearly 6000 feet of track, the train returns to the air-conditioned station.

Top: The 'lightning' paint scheme on the three trains is just one of several unique features of Desperado – which, in 1996, was the tallest complete-circuit roller coaster in North America.

Above: Buffalo Bill's is one of the few hotels in the world where you can wake up, and with the help of Desperado, tour the property at more than 70 mph.

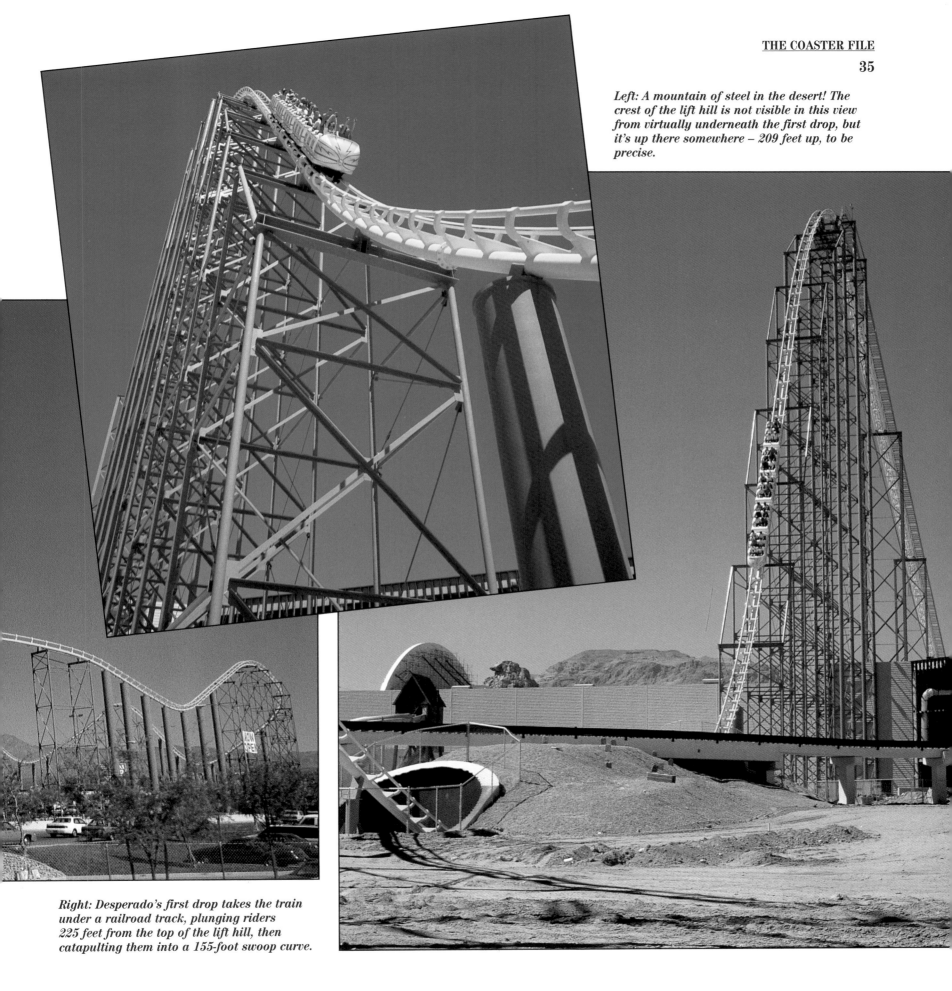

Left: A mountain of steel in the desert! The crest of the lift hill is not visible in this view from virtually underneath the first drop, but it's up there somewhere – 209 feet up, to be precise.

Right: Desperado's first drop takes the train under a railroad track, plunging riders 225 feet from the top of the lift hill, then catapulting them into a 155-foot swoop curve.

BATMAN THE RIDE

Above: Batman The Ride – the fourth coaster of its kind built at a Six Flags theme park, is a mirror-image of the first three.

LOCATION: Six Flags Over Mid-America, Eureka, Missouri, USA
YEAR BUILT: 1995
CONSTRUCTOR: Bolliger & Mabillard
MAXIMUM HEIGHT: 105 feet
LENGTH: 2693 feet
TOP SPEED: 50 mph
CAPACITY PER TRAIN: 32
LONGEST DROP: 80 feet
RIDE DURATION: 2 minutes
INVERSIONS: 5

After flinging eager guests screaming into the next century with wildly successful Batman The Ride installations at three of their other parks, Six Flags decided to go to the well again in 1995, but with an extra twist this time. Innovative designers Bolliger & Mabillard took the winning formula and built a *mirror image* Batman at Six Flags Over Mid-America. The result is the most inverted BTR yet.

Set amid the glamorous backdrop of the Time Warner Studios themed area, riders in 'ski-lift' style coaches experience close to four Gs of force as they are rocketed through five inversions: two outside vertical loops, two outside corkscrew turns and a zero gravity roll. The 2600-foot long track takes riders 105 feet in the air and measures 77 feet high at its tallest loop.

Left: Guests at Six Flags Over Mid-America, near St Louis, find themselves head over heels as they encounter one of the two outside corkscrew turns on Batman The Ride.

TIMBER WOLF

Above: Although it only appears to be lower than it actually is, a structural support like this usually causes everyone aboard to duck.

LOCATION: Worlds Of Fun, Kansas City, Missouri, USA
YEAR BUILT: 1989
CONSTRUCTOR: Dinn Corporation
MAXIMUM HEIGHT: 100 feet
LENGTH: 4230 feet
TOP SPEED: 53 mph
CAPACITY PER TRAIN: 24
LONGEST DROP: 95 feet
RIDE DURATION: 2 minutes 30 seconds
INVERSIONS: 0

Covering seven acres, the Timber Wolf features an exciting combination of speed, turns and drops during its breathtaking two and a half minute journey.

At the top of the 100-foot lift, the Timber Wolf turns left and plummets 95 feet at 50 degrees and 53 miles per hour, allowing riders to experience a 2.85 G-force. Maintaining its speed, the Timber Wolf slams through a high-banked left turn, crests a series of hills and valleys, races through the structure, through a helix and several hairpin turns before returning to the station.

Left: After climbing the 100-foot tall lift hill, fast turns and plenty of negative Gs highlight an exciting ride aboard Worlds Of Fun's Timber Wolf.

SCREAMIN' EAGLE

LOCATION: Six Flags Over Mid-America,
 Eureka, Missouri, USA
YEAR BUILT: 1976
CONSTRUCTOR: Philadelphia Toboggan Co.
MAXIMUM HEIGHT: 110 feet
LENGTH: 3872 feet
TOP SPEED: 62 mph
CAPACITY PER TRAIN: 24
LONGEST DROP: 92 feet
RIDE DURATION: 2 minutes 30 seconds
INVERSIONS: 0

Above: The Screamin' Eagle soars down its quarter-mile wooden track at speeds up to 62 miles per hour.

Similar in design to Atlanta's Great American Scream Machine, John Allen and the Philadelphia Toboggan Company engineered and built the Screamin' Eagle, a massive L-shaped out-and-back woodie measuring 3872 feet long. When it was constructed in 1976, the Eagle had the distinction of being the longest and tallest coaster in the world.

Right: The Screamin' Eagle's front seat gives riders a panoramic view of the graceful hills and sprawling structure of this classic John Allen woodie, built in 1976.

RAVEN

LOCATION: Holiday World, Santa Claus,
  Indiana, USA
YEAR BUILT: 1995
CONSTRUCTOR: Custom Coasters International
MAXIMUM HEIGHT: 110 feet
LENGTH: 2800 feet
TOP SPEED: 50 mph
CAPACITY PER TRAIN: 24

LONGEST DROP: 86 feet
RIDE DURATION: 1 minute 40 seconds
INVERSIONS: 0

Below: Secluded from the outside world in a wooded area, first-time Raven riders are delighted by the coaster's non-stop excitement and combination of high-speed transitions.

When Holiday World management decided to add a wooden coaster to their mix of attractions, they researched the project by traveling to other facilities to experience the best qualities of existing favorites. The resulting Raven is a hybrid of several proven elements from other popular North American thrillers. A steep drop into a dark tunnel, a 180-degree turn over a lake, a twisting track hidden deep in the woods, non-stop speed and plenty of out-of-your-seat action throughout the ride are just some of the highlights of this excellent coaster, built by CCI in 1995.

Below: Raven effectively combines some of the best elements from America's great woodies, including the tunnel, the wooded setting, and this scenic 180-degree turn over Lake Rudolph.

HOOSIER HURRICANE

LOCATION: Indiana Beach, Monticello,
  Indiana, USA
YEAR BUILT: 1994
CONSTRUCTOR: Custom Coasters International
MAXIMUM HEIGHT: 100 feet
LENGTH: 3000 feet
TOP SPEED: 55 mph
CAPACITY PER TRAIN: 24
LONGEST DROP: 90 feet
RIDE DURATION: 1 minute 30 seconds
INVERSIONS: 0

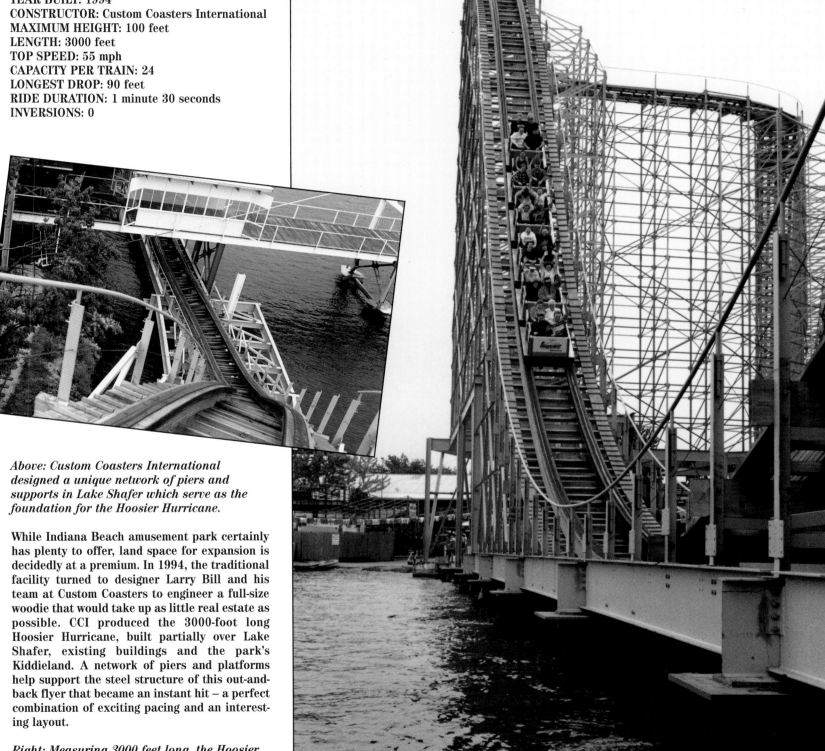

*Above: Custom Coasters International
designed a unique network of piers and
supports in Lake Shafer which serve as the
foundation for the Hoosier Hurricane.*

While Indiana Beach amusement park certainly
has plenty to offer, land space for expansion is
decidedly at a premium. In 1994, the traditional
facility turned to designer Larry Bill and his
team at Custom Coasters to engineer a full-size
woodie that would take up as little real estate as
possible. CCI produced the 3000-foot long
Hoosier Hurricane, built partially over Lake
Shafer, existing buildings and the park's
Kiddieland. A network of piers and platforms
help support the steel structure of this out-and-
back flyer that became an instant hit – a perfect
combination of exciting pacing and an interesting layout.

*Right: Measuring 3000 feet long, the Hoosier
Hurricane is the longest coaster in the state of
Indiana. The ride has become known for its
quick turns and breathtaking speed.*

OUTLAW

LOCATION: Adventureland Park, Des Moines,
 Iowa, USA
YEAR BUILT: 1993
CONSTRUCTOR: Custom Coasters International
MAXIMUM HEIGHT: 67 feet
LENGTH: 2800 feet
TOP SPEED: 48 mph
CAPACITY PER TRAIN: 24
LONGEST DROP: 65 feet
RIDE DURATION: 2 minutes
INVERSIONS: 0

*Right: Straight track is virtually non-existent
on Adventureland's Outlaw. Even the first
drop is curved! Here the swooping drops,
heavily-banked turns and 2800 feet of track
combine for a surprisingly smooth ride.
The six-car PTC trains are equipped only with
standard lap bars and no headrests, in
time-honored coaster tradition.*

One of the best examples of a wooden coaster
under 70 feet tall delivering maximum excitement for its relatively small size is
Adventureland's Outlaw. Built at the traditional
park in 1993 by Custom Coasters International
as the centerpiece of Adventureland's $5 million
twentieth anniversary expansion, the two-minute
ride features a total of twelve curves and nine
drops.

Outlaw's compact, twisting layout contains
almost no straight track, instead relying on raw
speed, smooth turns and transitions to entertain
its passengers. In height, the Outlaw is the short-
est of the Adventureland trio of coasters – the
90-foot tall steel double-looping Dragon, and the
93-foot tall out-and-back wooden Tornado are
the other thrillers-in-residence.

*Left: Standing only 67 feet high, Outlaw
proves that a coaster doesn't necessarily have
to be tall to be exciting.*

VORTEX

LOCATION: Paramount's Carowinds, Charlotte,
  North Carolina, USA
YEAR BUILT: 1992
CONSTRUCTOR: Bolliger & Mabillard
MAXIMUM HEIGHT: 90 feet
LENGTH: 2040 feet
TOP SPEED: 50 mph
CAPACITY PER TRAIN: 24
LONGEST DROP: 138 feet
RIDE DURATION: 2 minutes 30 seconds
INVERSIONS: 2

"We designed the Vortex to create a unique succession of exciting and unparalleled thrills, obtained by a rapid variation of the direction and amount of the acceleration acting on the human body," explains Walter Bolliger, metallurgist representing ride manufacturers Bolliger & Mabillard. The $5.5 million coaster features a 90-foot lift hill, into a vertical loop, an upward helix, down through a 'carousel formation,' a flat spin and a series of added lifts and drops, all performed while standing up. The ride is similar to the Vortex standing coaster at Paramount's Great America, Santa Clara, California.

Above: This convoluted track is a tribute to the engineering precision of B&M. The Vortex is the third standing coaster built by the Swiss firm.

Below: While speeding through more than 2000 feet of track standing up, riders encounter a series of inversions and dramatic turns.

TWISTER II

LOCATION: Elitch Gardens Amusement Park, Denver, Colorado, USA
YEAR BUILT: 1995
CONSTRUCTOR: John Pierce Assoc./Hensel Phelps
MAXIMUM HEIGHT: 100 feet
LENGTH: 3400 feet
TOP SPEED: 54 mph
CAPACITY PER TRAIN: 20
LONGEST DROP: 90 feet
RIDE DURATION: 2 minutes
INVERSIONS: 0

Forced to move to a new site because of space limitations, Denver's Elitch Gardens moved the entire park to a downtown location in 1995. Unfortunately, the park's classic John Allen-designed Twister coaster was left behind in the move, so a similar, but slightly modified version was constructed at the new park, adjacent to the city's Mile High Stadium.

The sister of Twister, designed by John Pierce Associates, stands 100 feet high, and was built to be a crowd-pleaser. Utilizing the trains from the original ride, Twister II zips through its curvy 3400 feet of track, highlighted by a banked, totally dark 250-foot long tunnel – one of the best on any coaster in the world. As the park's publicity says, its a "mountain of fun, right in the city."

Below: Riders seem nearly lost among the 10-story high superstructure of Twister II. An excellent dark tunnel and strong lateral Gs are among the coaster's highlights.

Bottom: Similar in layout to the 1964 original, Twister II debuted when the new Elitch Gardens amusement park opened in downtown Denver in 1995, using two trains from the original ride.

VORTEX

LOCATION: Paramount's Kings Island, Kings Island, Ohio, USA
YEAR BUILT: 1987
CONSTRUCTOR: Arrow Dynamics
MAXIMUM HEIGHT: 148 feet
LENGTH: 3800 feet
TOP SPEED: 50 mph
CAPACITY PER TRAIN: 28
LONGEST DROP: 138 feet
RIDE DURATION: 2 minutes 30 seconds
INVERSIONS: 6

Below: On the site originally occupied by Arrow's first suspended coaster, the Bat, Kings Island installed the $4 million Vortex, Arrow's first six-inversion coaster, in 1987.

A virtual showcase of Arrow Dynamics steel coaster elements, the Vortex at Paramount's Kings Island turns riders upside-down a total of six times during its disorienting two and a half minute journey.

Vortex riders climb a 148-foot lift hill, then drop 138 feet at a 55-degree angle into a hairpin turn that leads into two vertical loops (72 and 62 feet high, respectively), followed by a 200-foot long corkscrew, a 60-foot drop boomerang, and a 360-degree helix.

Right: It's easy to see why passengers tend to lose their sense of direction during the two and one-half minute ride on the 50 mph, multi-element Vortex!

The BEAST

LOCATION: Paramount"s Kings Island, Kings
  Island, Ohio, USA
YEAR BUILT: 1979
CONSTRUCTOR: Dinn/KECO
MAXIMUM HEIGHT: 135 feet
LENGTH: 7400 feet
TOP SPEED: 65 mph
CAPACITY PER TRAIN: 36
LONGEST DROP: 141 feet
RIDE DURATION: 4 minutes
INVERSIONS: 0

*Right: At Paramount's Kings Island, the
heavily-wooded setting of the Beast adds to
the anticipation of what lies ahead.*

*Far right, inset: The first of two lift hills on
the Beast, the longest wooden coaster in the
world. The ride covers 35 acres.*

*Below: With 7400 feet of track and a 540-degree
banked helix tunnel finale, many consider the
Beast to be the ultimate woodie experience.*

The Beast has been called every adjective in the book, from 'awesome' and 'terrifying' to 'ultimate' and 'legendary.' The one description that everyone agrees on is 'unforgettable.' First unchained on Friday, April 13, 1979, The Beast covers more than 35 acres of densely-wooded terrain and reigns as the longest wooden roller coaster on the planet. A single ride takes almost four minutes.

Constructed by a team led by Charles Dinn, The Beast was built in less than a year, after two years of planning and design. The first two-thirds of the ride is a fast-paced trip through a series of hills, turns and tunnels, but after a second lift hill, the big finish features a 141-foot long drop into a banked 540-degree helix tunnel.

Right: One of the highlights of a three-minute, forty-second Beast ride is this 135-foot first drop into a tunnel.

MAGNUM XL-200

LOCATION: Cedar Point, on a Lake Erie
  Peninsula, Sandusky, Ohio, USA
YEAR BUILT: 1989
CONSTRUCTOR: Arrow Dynamics
MAXIMUM HEIGHT: 205 feet
LENGTH: 5106 feet
TOP SPEED: 72 mph
CAPACITY PER TRAIN: 36
LONGEST DROP: 194 feet
RIDE DURATION: 2 minutes
INVERSIONS: 0

Below: Riders begin the 205-foot climb to the top of the Magnum XL-200 at Cedar Point, overlooking Lake Erie.

Right: Ranked by readers of Inside Track *as the world's best steel roller coaster, Magnum XL-200 reaches speeds of 72 mph.*

Built in 1989 by Arrow Dynamics, the Magnum XL-200 was the first full-circuit roller coaster in the world to break the elusive 200-foot tall plateau. Since that time, this massive steel ride has thrilled millions, and converted many skeptics who originally thought that a steel coaster had to include inversions to be fun. Anticipation builds during the Magnum's incredible 205-foot climb to the top of the first hill, then the speed builds to a blistering 72 miles per hour on the 195-foot drop off the other side. Riders get a one-of-a-kind view of Lake Erie over the next amazing hill, before turning left and blazing through a turnaround element and three 'rabbit-hop' tunnels with special effects.

Left: Returning to the station, these Magnum XL-200 riders enjoy a fast trip along the shore of Lake Erie.

MEAN STREAK

LOCATION: Cedar Point, on a Lake Erie
   Peninsula, Sandusky, Ohio, USA
YEAR BUILT: 1991
CONSTRUCTOR: Dinn Corporation
MAXIMUM HEIGHT: 161 feet
LENGTH: 5427 feet
TOP SPEED: 65 mph
CAPACITY PER TRAIN: 28
LONGEST DROP: 155 feet
RIDE DURATION: 2 minutes 20 seconds
INVERSIONS: 0

Right: The second-tallest structure on the awesome roller coaster skyline of Sandusky, Ohio, is the 161-foot tall Mean Streak. Behind it are two more of Cedar Point's twelve coasters – the wood structure/double steel track Gemini, and the Magnum XL-200.

Below: The queue lines for Cedar Point's Mean Streak are inside the structure of the coaster, so waiting guests can get a close-up look at the thrills that lie ahead!

MEAN STREAK

THE HEIGHT OF TERROR

With a track length measuring more than a mile, and a structure topping out at a height of 161 feet, the Mean Streak is one serious lumberyard. And with its 155-foot first drop, the ride ranks among an elite few for sheer excitement on the way down. Starting at Cedar Point's Frontiertown themed area, the coaster runs toward Sandusky Bay outside the perimeter of the park, repeating a figure-eight pattern three times both side by side and winding through itself.

Covering a footprint of nearly 5.5 acres and containing more than 1.5 million board feet of lumber, this landmark mega-coaster marked the final efforts of the design and construction team of Curtis D Summers and Charles Dinn.

Right: Verified by radar as traveling at 65 miles per hour, the Mean Streak ranks among the fastest wood coasters currently operating anywhere in the world.

RAPTOR

LOCATION: Cedar Point, on a Lake Erie
  Peninsula, Sandusky, Ohio, USA
YEAR BUILT: 1994
CONSTRUCTOR: Bolliger & Mabillard
MAXIMUM HEIGHT: 137 feet
LENGTH: 3790 feet
TOP SPEED: 57 mph
CAPACITY PER TRAIN: 32
LONGEST DROP: 119 feet
RIDE DURATION: 2 minutes 15 seconds
INVERSIONS: 6

Cedar Point's eleventh roller coaster project, this spectacular suspended, outside-looping coaster represented an park investment of $12 million. Opened on May 27, 1994, its six inversions comprise one vertical 360-degree loop, three barrel rolls, and one 'cobra' roll which turns riders upside-down twice - the first use of this type of element on a suspended looping coaster. Ride height is fifty-four inches or over, in ski-lift style seating with shoulder harness and lap belt, arranged four abreast.

Far Left: The first element after the initial drop is Raptor's 100 foot tall vertical loop.

Left: One of three 360-degree barrel rolls which the cars take at speeds of over fifty miles an hour.

Left: Raptor's unique cobra roll turns riders upside-down twice, flipping over and into a 180-degree roll, before repeating the movement on the way out.

Above: 300 columns support the tubular steel track. Thirty-two riders sit four abreast, legs dangling free. The attraction handles 1800 riders per hour.

GEORGIA CYCLONE

LOCATION: Six Flags Over Georgia, Atlanta,
 Georgia, USA
YEAR BUILT: 1990
CONSTRUCTOR: Dinn Corporation
MAXIMUM HEIGHT: 95 feet
LENGTH: 2970 feet
TOP SPEED: 50 mph
CAPACITY PER TRAIN: 24
LONGEST DROP: 78 feet
RIDE DURATION: 1 minute 48 seconds
INVERSIONS: 0

Above: 50 miles per hour is the top speed of Atlanta's Georgia Cyclone. The ride includes 11 drops and features high-banked turns.

There are now five imitations of the original Coney Island Cyclone operating at different parks worldwide (four of which were built at Six Flags locations), but the Georgia Cyclone consistently ranks among the best of the clones. One ride on this Atlanta scream machine and you'll have Georgia on your mind for some time to come. Built by the Curtis D Summers and Charles Dinn team in 1990, this version is a mirror image of the New York ride with some slight modifications. The structure is ten feet taller, the track is a bit longer, and the coaster begins with a shorter initial drop. The alterations prove to be a benefit: the PTC cars fly through the turns and down the steep drops at speeds reaching 50 miles per hour, guaranteeing some good air time on many of the hills. Additionally, Six Flags Over Georgia features another popular wood coaster, the Great American Scream Machine.

Left: The complex structure of the Georgia Cyclone, designed by Curtis D Summers, was completed in 1990, and contains nearly 3000 feet of track.

Left, inset: The 53-degree first drop is a mirror-image of the original Coney Island Cyclone, which is featured on page 74.

GREEZED LIGHTNIN'

LOCATION: Six Flags AstroWorld, Houston, Texas, USA
YEAR BUILT: 1978
CONSTRUCTOR: Intamin AG
MAXIMUM HEIGHT: 138 feet
LENGTH: 849 feet
TOP SPEED: 55 mph
CAPACITY PER TRAIN: 28
HEIGHT OF LOOP: 76 feet
RIDE DURATION: 35 seconds
INVERSIONS 2 (1 forward, 1 backward)

A popular ride for many parks in the late 1970s and early 1980s, many of the original shuttle loop coasters are beginning to disappear from the scene. Fortunately, those that are still operating have been among the best all along, and Greezed Lightnin' remains Houston's favorite rocket. The shuttle loop features one (for obvious reasons) seven-car train that is catapulted out of the station, and down a straight section of track where it travels through a 76-foot high loop. After the loop, the track angles skyward

Above: Constructed in 1978, Greezed Lightnin' remains one of the most thrilling shuttle loop coasters in the world today. The ride is one of nine roller coasters at Houston's AstroWorld.

and ends. The train climbs most of the way up, loses momentum and falls back down, repeating the sequence backward and speeding through the loading station. At the far end of the track, another section of angled track catches the train, returning it to the station brakes.

RATTLER

LOCATION: Six Flags Fiesta Texas,
  San Antonio, Texas, USA
YEAR BUILT: 1992
CONSTRUCTOR: Roller Coaster Corp. of America
MAXIMUM HEIGHT: 176 feet
LENGTH: 5080 feet
TOP SPEED: 55 mph
CAPACITY PER TRAIN: 28
LONGEST DROP: 124 feet
RIDE DURATION: 2 minutes 10 seconds
INVERSIONS: 0

Although it officially remains the tallest wooden coaster in the world at 176 feet, the Rattler has undergone a series of structural modifications during its short lifetime that have somewhat mellowed its record-shattering statistics. The incredible 166-foot long first drop off the side of a rock cliff has bee lessened to 124 feet, while

Above: Riders hang on for the start of Rattler's first drop – 124 feet down the side of a natural rock cliff. The coaster travels a total distance of 5080 feet.

Left: The sprawling Rattler effectively utilizes the terrain of the rock quarry in which the Six Flags Fiesta Texas theme park is located.

similar alterations have been made to the Rattler's fan curve, helix, second drop and station fly-by trackage. Even the original trains have been replaced with coaches from Philadelphia Toboggan Company. Nonetheless, the Rattler continues to shine as the park's only woodie, highlighted by the two initial drops and a passage into a tunnel actually cut through the limestone quarry wall.

Below: Two thrilling drops, a triple helix and a natural rock tunnel are among the features of the world's tallest wooden coaster.

TEXAS GIANT

Below: An excellent on-board view back to the lift hill and first drop. A speed of over sixty miles per hour is attained at this point, as the train heads for a swooping left turn.

LOCATION: Six Flags Over Texas, Arlington, Texas, USA
YEAR BUILT: 1990
CONSTRUCTOR: Six Flags Over Texas
MAXIMUM HEIGHT: 143 feet
LENGTH: 4920 feet
TOP SPEED: 62 mph
CAPACITY PER TRAIN: 28
LONGEST DROP: 137 feet
RIDE DURATION: 2 minutes
INVERSIONS 0

Above: Riders prepare for one of the twenty-one drops, aboard the Texas Giant's seven-car train.

Six Flags Over Texas was named for the flags which have flown over Texas in the past, namely Spain, France, Mexico, The Confederacy, The Republic of Texas and The United States. It was the first in the chain of Six Flags parks, opening the gates to its 205 acres in 1961.

This 143 foot tall coaster was the third tallest woodie in the world in 1996. A top speed of 62 miles per hour is achieved off the first hill by virtue of its 137 foot drop at a 53 degree angle. Designer Curtis D Summers incorporated no less than twenty-one drops into the circuit, in honor of it being his twenty-first design.

Right: A panoramic view of a spectacular ride; Texas Giant has consistently featured in coaster enthusiasts' lists of their top ten rides.
Right, inset: The train is dwarfed by the mountain of timber supporting the first hill.

KUMBA

LOCATION: Busch Gardens Tampa Bay, Tampa,
 Florida, USA
YEAR BUILT: 1993
CONSTRUCTOR: Bolliger & Mabillard
MAXIMUM HEIGHT: 143 feet
LENGTH: 3978 feet
TOP SPEED: 63 mph
CAPACITY PER TRAIN: 32
LONGEST DROP: 135 feet
RIDE DURATION: 2 minutes 54 seconds
INVERSIONS: 7

The 143-foot tall Kumba, from the African word meaning 'roar,' is the second-tallest roller coaster in the South-Eastern United States, topped only by its inverted sister, Montu. Designed and built by Bolliger & Mabillard, the multi-million dollar maze of spectacular turquoise-colored track features a 'diving loop,' a camelback, a 'cobra roll' around a spectator bridge, a vertical spiral and a 108-foot tall vertical loop (one of the world's largest) – highlighting an assortment of elements adding up to seven inversions on nearly 4000 feet of twisted track. Riders sit four-across in eight cars and reach speeds of up to 63 miles per hour.

Below: Kumba, the second-tallest roller coaster in the southeastern United States, dominates the skyline at Busch Gardens Tampa Bay, Florida.

Right: Innovative trains hold 32 passengers seated four-across for a wild ride on Kumba that lasts just under three minutes.

Far right: A 108-foot vertical loop is just one of several spectacular elements that highlight Kumba at Florida's Busch Gardens.

SPACE MOUNTAIN

LOCATION: Magic Kingdom at Walt Disney World, Lake Buena Vista, Florida, USA
YEAR BUILT: 1975
CONSTRUCTOR: WED
MAXIMUM HEIGHT: 90 feet
LENGTH: Alpha track 3186 feet
      Omega track 3196 feet
TOP SPEED: 29 mph
CAPACITY PER TRAIN: 6
RIDE DURATION: 2 minutes 30 seconds
INVERSIONS: 0

Opened in 1975 after a decade in development, Florida's Space Mountain cost more to build than the entire Disneyland theme park in California twenty years earlier.

Located in the Tomorrowland section, and one of three excellent 'mountain' attractions at Disney's Magic Kingdom, this simulated trip through space consists of two separate steel coasters enclosed in a cone-shaped building the size of a football field. While not exceptionally fast, a ride on Space Mountain *feels* like it is much quicker because riders are surrounded in total darkness, punctuated only by occasional special effects and lighting. After a short count-down, space explorers rocket through the 'universe' in two-car, three-seat vehicles. The whole experience lasts two and a half minutes from launch to 're-entry.'

Left: Guests prepare for launch on Space Mountain, a dual-track indoor coaster.

Below: Two separate complete-circuit steel coasters in the dark are inside the Magic Kingdom's Space Mountain building.

WILD ONE

LOCATION: Adventure World, Largo, Maryland, USA
YEAR BUILT: 1986
CONSTRUCTOR: Dinn Corporation
MAXIMUM HEIGHT: 98 feet
LENGTH: 4000 feet
TOP SPEED: 53 mph
CAPACITY PER TRAIN: 20
LONGEST DROP: 88 feet
RIDE DURATION: 2 minutes 30 seconds
INVERSIONS: 0

Hold on! This out-and-back woodie is one wild machine. Built in 1917 as the Giant Coaster at Paragon Park in Massachusetts, it was a favorite of New Englanders for decades. The beachfront park closed in 1985 and the coaster was auctioned after the season. Management at Wild World (now Adventure World) searching for a signature ride to anchor their expanding amusement section, purchased the Giant and moved it to Maryland, where it was renamed and rebuilt under the supervision of Charles Dinn. A 520-degree helix, destroyed by fire in the early 1960s, was reconstructed.

Top: Wild One was originally the Giant Coaster at Paragon Park in Massachusetts. It was purchased at auction in 1985 and relocated to Maryland, where it opened the following year.

Right: Originally, Wild One's first drop went all the way to the ground, but was shortened by nine feet during some reprofiling before the 1992 season.

GRIZZLY

Above: Almost completely secluded by the dense woods at the back of Kings Dominion, the Grizzly hides many of its exciting features until seconds before riders encounter them.

LOCATION: Paramount's Kings Dominion,
  Doswell, Virginia, USA
YEAR BUILT: 1982
CONSTRUCTOR: Taft Attractions Group
MAXIMUM HEIGHT: 87 feet
LENGTH: 3150 feet
TOP SPEED: 50 mph
CAPACITY PER TRAIN: 28
LONGEST DROP: 85 feet
RIDE DURATION: 2 minutes 10 seconds
INVERSIONS: 0

With its design based on the classic Wildcat coaster that once thrilled guests at Cincinnati, Ohio's Coney Island, and its location hidden deep in a wooded corner of Kings Dominion, the 87-foot tall Grizzly is nearly completely enshrouded in trees.

The 3150-foot long woodie incorporates a modified double out-and-back layout to deliver a frenzied ride through the forest. A noisy tunnel adds to the excitement, but the Grizzly is best when ridden in the dark.

Left: Many of the twists and turns on the Grizzly are neatly disguised, as riders cannot see the track beyond the next drop.

ANACONDA

LOCATION: Paramount's Kings Dominion,
  Doswell, Virginia, USA
YEAR BUILT: 1991
CONSTRUCTOR: Arrow Dynamics
MAXIMUM HEIGHT: 128 feet
LENGTH: 2700 feet
TOP SPEED: 50 mph
CAPACITY PER TRAIN: 28
LONGEST DROP: 144 feet
RIDE DURATION: 2 minutes 10 seconds
INVERSIONS: 4

Built on the site originally occupied by the King Cobra shuttle loop coaster, Kings Dominion's winding steel Anaconda was installed in 1991 and is positioned almost entirely over Lake Charles.

After a 128-foot climb up the lift hill, the green seven-car train turns right and begins its journey over the water, diving into a 144-foot drop through a short tunnel below the water line, then back up into two loops, a one-of-a kind non-inversion butterfly element and a corkscrew. The 2700-foot long ride was custom-designed and built by Arrow Dynamics, and sits alongside the park's white racing woodie, Rebel Yell.

Top: Built almost entirely over (and in) Lake Charles, Anaconda turns riders upside-down at a speed of 50 miles per hour.

Above: From across the lake, Anaconda appears to dive into the water. In reality it runs through a short underwater tunnel.

DRACHEN FIRE

LOCATION: Busch Gardens Williamsburg,
 Williamsburg, Virginia, USA
YEAR BUILT: 1992
CONSTRUCTOR: Arrow Dynamics
MAXIMUM HEIGHT: 150 feet
LENGTH: 3550 feet
TOP SPEED: 61 mph
CAPACITY PER TRAIN: 28
LONGEST DROP: 130 feet
RIDE DURATION: 2 minutes 25 seconds
INVERSIONS: 5

Left: Drachen Fire was the first roller coaster to utilize the 'bat wing' element. Passengers are turned upside-down a total of five times on this coaster.

Above: About 355,000 pounds of steel were used to construct the electric-blue colored Drachen Fire track. Only part of the track can be seen from the loading station, adding to the anticipation of the ride.

The 150-foot tall Drachen Fire ('Drachen' is German for 'Dragon') showcased a number of new twists for Arrow Dynamics when it debuted in 1992, including sleek, aerodynamic cars with 'flaming' paint scheme; a 'wraparound corkscrew' followed by a spiraling dive to the ground; a camelback hump; a boomerang-like 'batwing' which rolls passengers upside-down twice, and a 'cutback' element that rotates the cars upside-down in a loop.

LOCH NESS MONSTER

LOCATION: Busch Gardens Williamsburg,
  Williamsburg, Virginia, USA
YEAR BUILT: 1978
CONSTRUCTOR: Arrow Development
MAXIMUM HEIGHT: 130 feet
LENGTH: 3240 feet
TOP SPEED: 60 mph
CAPACITY PER TRAIN: 28
LONGEST DROP: 114 feet
RIDE DURATION: 2 minutes 10 seconds
INVERSIONS: 2

Built three years after Busch Gardens opened, this popular coaster is located in the Scotland-themed area of the park called 'Heatherdowns.' Constructed over a manmade lake, the ride is highlighted by interlocking 360-degree loops. The cars accelerate to the ride's top speed of 60 miles per hour on the 114-foot first drop, creating a G-force of 3.5 in the process. Between the loops, the train negotiates a spiral track through a dark tunnel containing special effects. Spectacular views of the ride can be obtained from the skyway gondolas which cruise alongside.

Left: Virginia's Loch Ness Monster, with its 114-foot drop over the water, has become a favorite among steel coaster lovers.

Above: On days when Busch Gardens is operating all three trains on Nessie, two will cross paths on the interlocking loops.

THUNDERBOLT

LOCATION: Kennywood Park, West Mifflin,
 Pennsylvania, USA
YEAR BUILT: 1924 (reconfigured in 1968)
CONSTRUCTOR: Miller/Vettel
MAXIMUM HEIGHT: 70 feet
LENGTH: 2887 feet
TOP SPEED: 55 mph
CAPACITY PER TRAIN: 24
LONGEST DROP: 98 feet
RIDE DURATION: 1 minute 30 seconds
INVERSIONS: 0

*Left: Fast turns and surprise heart-pounding
drops are the highlights of a ride aboard
Kennywood's classic Thunderbolt woodie.*

Ranking among the world's best examples of a
terrain-coaster, the popular Thunderbolt is full
of surprises, thanks in part to its hillside location. The ravine sections of the superstructure
were saved from its predecessor, the Pippin,
which was designed by John Miller and built in
1924. In 1968, designer Andy Vettel incorporated
new hills and curves on the elevated area above
the existing coaster, enabling the Thunderbolt
to travel up and down the hillside, with the
unusual feature of the chain lift at the end.

*Below: The Thunderbolt has been delivering
thrilling rides since 1924. The historic N.A.D.
trains were originally equipped with headlights.*

STEEL PHANTOM

LOCATION: Kennywood Park, West Mifflin,
  Pennsylvania, USA
YEAR BUILT: 1991
CONSTRUCTOR: Arrow Dynamics
MAXIMUM HEIGHT: 160 feet
LENGTH: 3000 feet
TOP SPEED: 80 mph
CAPACITY PER TRAIN: 28
LONGEST DROP: 225 feet
RIDE DURATION: 2 minutes 15 seconds
INVERSIONS: 4

It's not a ghost, but it moves just as fast. The $4.5 million Steel Phantom has been clocked at speeds exceeding 75 miles per hour. The ride's towering 160-foot lift hill leads to an intense 157-foot curving first drop banked at 63 degrees. But it's the Phantom's second drop that breaks distance records, plunging 225 feet through the wooden structure of Kennywood's Thunderbolt coaster. Upon reaching the bottom of the hill, the train makes a swooping left turn up a grade behind the Thunderbolt, launching into a vertical loop, butterfly boomerang element and half-corkscrew before hitting the brakes.

Above: Steel Phantom breaks Pennsylvania's posted speed limit, timed on radar traveling well above 75 miles per hour. It is one of four excellent coasters at Kennywood.

Top: The 160-foot tall Steel Phantom boasts the longest drop of any continuous-circuit coaster in the world – 225 feet – and its track slices through the structure of Thunderbolt.

HERCULES

LOCATION: Dorney Park & Wildwater
  Kingdom, Allentown, Pennsylvania, USA
YEAR BUILT: 1989
CONSTRUCTOR: Dinn Corporation
MAXIMUM HEIGHT: 95 feet
LENGTH: 4000 feet
TOP SPEED: 65 mph
CAPACITY PER TRAIN: 24
LONGEST DROP: 157 feet
RIDE DURATION: 2 minutes 10 seconds
INVERSIONS: 0

Using the hillside terrain to its full advantage, the Dinn Corporation was able to construct an outrageous drop over Dorney Park's lake without the need for building a huge lift hill. And unlike many coasters where the first drop is the longest, the big hill on Hercules is the second one – a world record 157-foot plunge, longest of any wooden coaster to date. When riders finally make it to the bottom, the track makes a sweeping right turn and climbs back up the side of the hill to begin the second half of the ride.

Top: Although the lift hill stands only 95 feet high, Hercules takes advantage of the terrain and drops riders 157 feet down to the lake. The track round the lake turn is banked at up to 55 degrees.

Right: Considered one of the most exhilarating drops of any coaster in the world, everyone holds on as Dorney Park's Hercules plummets at high speed down this 157-foot hill.

PHOENIX

LOCATION: Knoebels Amusement Resort,
  Elysburg, Pennsylvania, USA
YEAR BUILT: 1985
CONSTRUCTOR: Charles Dinn
MAXIMUM HEIGHT: 78 feet
LENGTH: 2300 feet
TOP SPEED: 45 mph
CAPACITY PER TRAIN: 24
LONGEST DROP: 73 feet
RIDE DURATION: 2 minutes 10 seconds
INVERSIONS: 0

Another coaster successfully rescued from a
defunct park, the Rocket at Joyland Park in San
Antonio, Texas, was disassembled and rebuilt as
the Phoenix at Knoebels Amusement Resort in
Pennsylvania during the winter of 1984-85.
Those who rode it in both locations say that the
ride actually improved in the process. The flight
on the Phoenix begins with a long, dark tunnel
before the lift hill, then continues through a
succession of rabbit hops and fast turns.

*Top: Once known as the Rocket at Joyland
Amusement Park in Texas, the reborn Phoenix
now operates at Knoebels Amusement Resort.*

*Right: In addition to sustained high speeds,
the Phoenix offers another treat: a rare
double-up and double-down track combination.*

RIVERSIDE CYCLONE

Above: Designer William Cobb's most terrifying coaster, the Riverside Cyclone became an instant favorite when it debuted in 1983.

Left: The remarkably tight structural design of the Riverside Cyclone conceals much of its twisting 3400 feet of track.

LOCATION: Riverside Park, Agawam,
  Massachusetts, USA
YEAR BUILT: 1983
CONSTRUCTOR: William Cobb Associates
MAXIMUM HEIGHT: 107 feet
LENGTH: 3400 feet
TOP SPEED: 60 mph
CAPACITY PER TRAIN: 24
LONGEST DROP: 70 feet
RIDE DURATION: 2 minutes
INVERSIONS: 0

Some attribute the ferocity of the Riverside Cyclone to the fact that designer William Cobb underwent heart surgery while he was designing the ride. Others point out that the coaster is packed into a small footprint, forcing the layout to require tight turns and rapid changes in direction. Whatever the reasons, the Cyclone provides one of the most exciting 'out-of-control' coaster ride experiences in North America. Its twisting configuration keeps riders guessing right from the first steeply-banked drop. Moving inward, hidden sections toward the center of the ride are filled with surprise drops, violent turns and plenty of air time.

Right: Riders get a glimpse of things to come from the top of the 107-foot lift hill as the Riverside Cyclone begins its high-speed journey back to the station.

PREDATOR

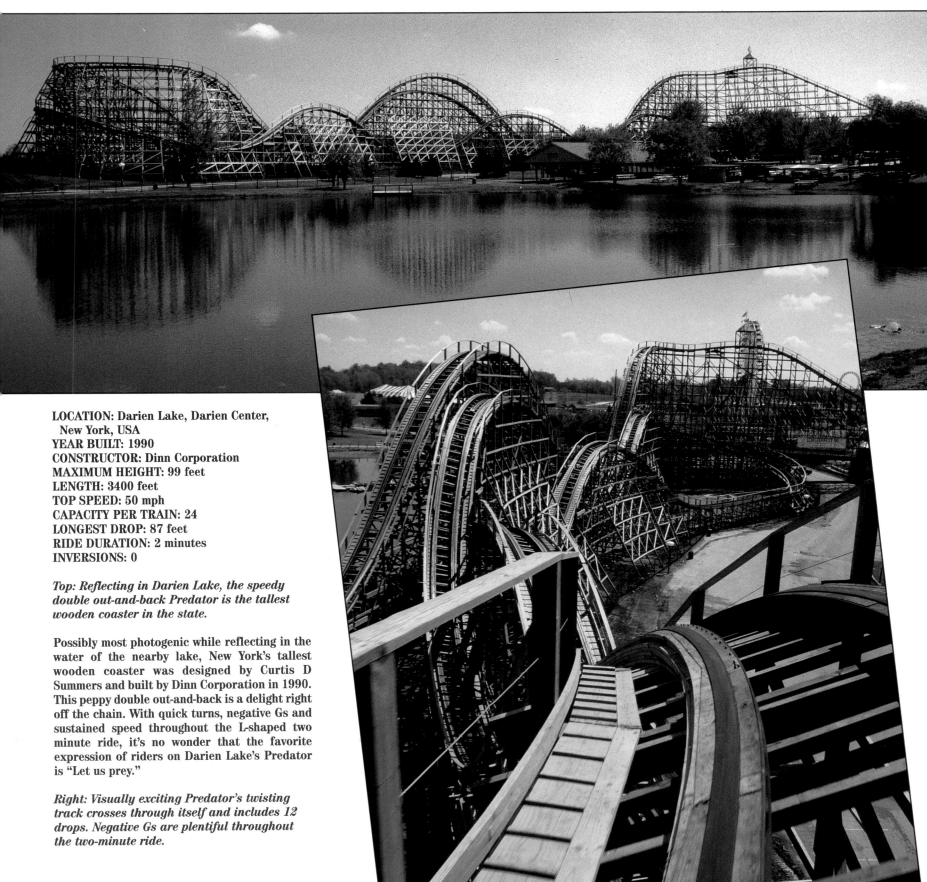

LOCATION: Darien Lake, Darien Center,
  New York, USA
YEAR BUILT: 1990
CONSTRUCTOR: Dinn Corporation
MAXIMUM HEIGHT: 99 feet
LENGTH: 3400 feet
TOP SPEED: 50 mph
CAPACITY PER TRAIN: 24
LONGEST DROP: 87 feet
RIDE DURATION: 2 minutes
INVERSIONS: 0

*Top: Reflecting in Darien Lake, the speedy
double out-and-back Predator is the tallest
wooden coaster in the state.*

Possibly most photogenic while reflecting in the
water of the nearby lake, New York's tallest
wooden coaster was designed by Curtis D
Summers and built by Dinn Corporation in 1990.
This peppy double out-and-back is a delight right
off the chain. With quick turns, negative Gs and
sustained speed throughout the L-shaped two
minute ride, it's no wonder that the favorite
expression of riders on Darien Lake's Predator
is "Let us prey."

*Right: Visually exciting Predator's twisting
track crosses through itself and includes 12
drops. Negative Gs are plentiful throughout
the two-minute ride.*

CYCLONE

LOCATION: Astroland Amusement Park,
 Coney Island, Brooklyn, New York, USA
YEAR BUILT: 1927
CONSTRUCTOR: Harry Baker/Vernon Keenan
MAXIMUM HEIGHT: 85 feet
LENGTH: 2640 feet
TOP SPEED: 50 mph
CAPACITY PER TRAIN: 24
LONGEST DROP: 85 feet
RIDE DURATION: 1 minute 50 seconds
INVERSIONS: 0

Below: The New York Times *once referred to the Cyclone as "a landmark for fear, joy and exhilaration." The first drop is steeply angled at 60 degrees, thrilling even seasoned riders.*

Still going strong after more than 65 years, the legendary Cyclone is regarded as the most famous roller coaster of them all. Along with the nearby Wonder Wheel and Parachute Drop, it's a New York City Landmark, and for good reason. Proudly situated on a street corner in Brooklyn, the Cyclone has attracted eager riders from all over the world. A Cyclone ride starts with a steeply banked first drop built all the way to the ground, and continues through several bone-jarring drops and violent turns before rounding one last slamming curve to return into the station. Among its many unique features, the Cyclone is the only coaster in America where you can re-ride

in the seat of your choice as long as you have the nerve (and of course, the cash). Some years ago, a man who was mute from birth rode the Cyclone. Following the ride, he staggered off the train and astounded onlookers by uttering the first three words of his life: "I feel sick."

Below: The popular Coney Island Cyclone coasts on a wooden track supported by a steel structure. The attraction was declared a New York City Landmark in July 1988.

COMET

LOCATION: The Great Escape, Lake George,
New York, USA
YEAR BUILT: 1994
CONSTRUCTOR: Philadelphia Toboggan Co.
MAXIMUM HEIGHT: 95 feet
LENGTH: 4197 feet
TOP SPEED: 55 mph
CAPACITY PER TRAIN: 24
LONGEST DROP: 87 feet
RIDE DURATION: 2 minutes
INVERSIONS: 0

Here's a long-running favorite that was moved not only to a different *park*, but an entirely different *country*. The Comet had an illustrious predecessor – it was built on the site of the legendary Crystal Beach Cyclone, considered by many the most ferocious ride in coaster history. The Comet was designed by Herb Schmeck and built by the Philadelphia Toboggan Company in 1948 on the shoreline of Lake Erie at Crystal Beach Amusement Park near Niagara Falls, Ontario, Canada. When the park closed in 1989,

many coaster aficionados thought that this great double out-and-back woodie might be lost forever. But in 1994, the Comet was moved from lakefront to Lake George, New York – specifically the Great Escape amusement park where it was rebuilt, and now performs better than ever.

Below: Originally the Crystal Beach Comet, and located outside Niagara Falls, Ontario until it closed in 1989, this ride made the transition to its present New York location in 1994.

The GREAT NOR'EASTER

LOCATION: Morey's Pier, Wildwood, New Jersey, USA
YEAR BUILT: 1995
CONSTRUCTOR: Vekoma International
MAXIMUM HEIGHT: 115 feet
LENGTH: 2170 feet
TOP SPEED: 55 mph
CAPACITY PER TRAIN: 20
LONGEST DROP: 95 feet
RIDE DURATION: 2 minutes 5 seconds
INVERSIONS: 5

Left: Every inch of real estate is valuable on Morey's Pier, so water slides and other attractions weave throughout the twisted steel structure of the Great Nor'Easter.

One of five Vekoma International suspended looping coasters that took North America by storm in 1995, The Great Nor'Easter is unique because of its location on Wildwood's Morey's Pier just a few hundred feet from the Atlantic Ocean.

Passengers get a close-up view of the beach as they ride two-by-two in ten rows of ski-lift style seats suspended from an overhead track. Not only does the actual ride deliver a rapid-fire sequence of breathtaking elements that turn passengers upside-down five times, but the trackage is positioned over and around several water slides, a lazy river, a log flume and sections of a waterpark. The Great Nor'Easter is named for the violent storms that historically ravage the east coast during the winter months.

Left: Named for the devastating weather phenomenon that periodically ravages the Mid-Atlantic coast, the Great Nor'Easter stormed into Wildwood, New Jersey in 1995.

Below: Passengers appear to be flying perilously close to the support columns, several water attractions and a log flume, enhancing the already thrilling experience.

Below: Two-across seating on the Great Nor'Easter gives every rider a great view of the Atlantic Ocean, even if it is upside-down.

SERPENT OF FIRE

LOCATION: La Feria Chapultepec Magico,
 Mexico City, Mexico
YEAR BUILT: 1964
CONSTRUCTOR: NAD
MAXIMUM HEIGHT: 110 feet
LENGTH: 4000 feet
TOP SPEED: 48 mph
CAPACITY PER TRAIN: 24
LONGEST DROP: 80 feet
RIDE DURATION: 3 minutes 15 seconds
INVERSIONS: 0

The most significant ride ever built by National Amusement Device, the massive 110-foot tall Serpent Of Fire (formerly known as La Montaña Rusa) stood as the tallest coaster in the world for more than a decade. Although it appears to be a twin-track coaster, Edward Leis designed the Serpent as one *continuous* track, so riders return to the station on the 'opposite' track to the one they left on.

The ride dominates the 15-acre La Feria park, and is painted in the colors of the Mexican flag. The station features an elaborate Aztec calendar on the ceiling.

Above: La Feria Chapultepec Magico is dominated by Serpent Of Fire, which gives riders a bird's-eye view of Mexico City.

Below: Colorful, themed trains carry passengers aboard Mexico City's huge Serpent Of Fire, originally known as La Montana Rusa.

ROLLER COASTER

LOCATION: Playland Amusement Park,
  Vancouver, British Columbia, Canada
YEAR BUILT: 1958
CONSTRUCTOR: Carl Phare
MAXIMUM HEIGHT: 69 feet
LENGTH: 2840 feet
TOP SPEED: 47 mph
CAPACITY PER TRAIN: 32
LONGEST DROP: 68 feet
RIDE DURATION: 1 minute 52 seconds
INVERSIONS: 0

*Below: The unique wraparound layout of the
Roller Coaster results in a ride that seems to
increase in speed as it travels along more
than a half-mile of track.*

Other than its name, everything about Playland's Roller Coaster is exciting and fun. Designed by Carl Phare and opening in 1958, this traditional treasure features an ever-tightening twisting layout and excellent pacing throughout the entire journey. Skillful operators cycle three sets of trains, each consisting of eight classic cars with fixed lap bars. There's plenty of air time on this speedy multi-level circuit, and Vancouver's picturesque mountain backdrop makes a ride truly unforgettable.

*Right: Classic coaster cars, non-stop speed
and plenty of air time are a few of the main
attractions of the Roller Coaster at Vancouver's
Playland, a ride built in the late fifties.*

DRAGON MOUNTAIN

LOCATION: Marineland, Niagara Falls,
 Ontario, Canada
YEAR BUILT: 1983
CONSTRUCTOR: Arrow/Huss
MAXIMUM HEIGHT: 186 feet
LENGTH: 5500 feet
TOP SPEED: 50 mph
CAPACITY PER TRAIN: 28
RIDE DURATION: 3 minutes 12 seconds
INVERSIONS: 4

Although it is one of the longest steel coasters in
the world, Dragon Mountain is memorable for
its odd components (and a few that never mate-
rialized). A large dragon mouth serves as the
entrance to the cavernous loading station. The
coaster's seemingly endless 186-foot double-
chainlift hill transports riders to the apex of the
manmade mountain, and, following a double
loop, meanders through steel supports where a
one-third scale replica of Niagara Falls and a
volcano were originally planned but never built.
The ride culminates in a long, dark tunnel lead-
ing to a startling 'bowtie' element, and back into
the station.

*Below: Brightly painted trains illustrate the
fire-breathing theme of Marineland's Dragon
Mountain, one of the longest and
tallest steel roller coasters in
North America.*

*Bottom: The Dragon loading station is visible
some distance beyond the coaster's bowtie
element.*

MINDBENDER

LOCATION: Galaxyland, West Edmonton Mall, Edmonton, Alberta, Canada
YEAR BUILT: 1985
CONSTRUCTOR: Schwarzkopf
MAXIMUM HEIGHT: 145 feet
LENGTH: 4198 feet
TOP SPEED: 45 mph
CAPACITY PER TRAIN: 12
LONGEST DROP: 125 feet
RIDE DURATION: 1 minute 13 seconds
INVERSIONS: 3

For anyone who feels the need to 'shop 'til you drop,' West Edmonton Mall can supply big doses of both. There are over 800 shops, but what about the drops? Those on Mindbender are among the most intense on any coaster in the world. The ride is located at one end of the indoor Galaxyland amusement park, so bad weather is not even a factor.

One of the most extreme roller coasters in the Schwarzkopf catalog, this triple-looping powerhouse delivers 5.2 Gs of excitement. Mindbender's structure stands more than fourteen stories tall, combining 4198 feet of track and near-vertical drops with a top speed of 45 miles per hour. Definitely not a ride for the beginner!

Top: Even the weather can't slow down the Mindbender, which races through 4198 feet of track at speeds of 45 miles per hour indoors.

Right: Entrance 10 to West Edmonton Mall brings shoppers face-to-face with the triple-looping Mindbender coaster, standing fourteen stories high.

VORTEX

LOCATION: Paramount Canada's Wonderland,
  Maple, Ontario, Canada
YEAR BUILT: 1991
CONSTRUCTOR: Arrow Dynamics
MAXIMUM HEIGHT: 97 feet
LENGTH: 2361 feet
TOP SPEED: 56 mph
CAPACITY PER TRAIN: 24
LONGEST DROP: 86 feet
RIDE DURATION: 1 minute 30 seconds
INVERSIONS: 0

Right: Wonder Mountain serves as the backdrop for Vortex, one of the most exciting of its type ever built by Arrow, and record-holder for North America's longest suspended coaster drop. Swinging widely from side to side as they make their 56 mph descent, the cars give passengers a real feeling of flying.

Left: Riders experience real thrills aboard Vortex among the picturesque surroundings of Canada's Wonderland. After diving off the mountainside, Vortex makes this wide right turn over Lake LeBarge, then takes several twists and turns and one more drop before returning to the station.

Between 1981 and 1993, Arrow Dynamics built ten suspended coasters for six parks in the USA, one in England (see pages 20-21), one in Japan, one in Korea, and one in Canada. Seventh in the series, the Vortex is among the most animated of them all, soaring and diving like an eagle from the top of Canada's Wonderland's Wonder Mountain.

The four-passenger cars swoop down the 86-foot drop at 56 miles per hour, then swing sideways to their fullest extent throughout much of the second half of the 2361-foot flight.

After a high-speed right turn over Lake LeBarge, the track curves up and over the lift hill and the loading station before dropping 73 feet and negotiating a few more curves, finally swinging into the brake run.

SKYRIDER

LOCATION: Paramount Canada's Wonderland, Maple, Ontario, Canada
YEAR BUILT: 1985
CONSTRUCTOR: TOGO Japan
MAXIMUM HEIGHT: 95 feet
LENGTH: 2231 feet
TOP SPEED: 50 mph
CAPACITY PER TRAIN: 24
LONGEST DROP: 92 feet
RIDE DURATION: 2 minutes
INVERSIONS: 1

Here's a ride where TOGO gets a standing ovation every time a train leaves the station. This Skyrider was the third in a series of standing coasters with similar layouts (others operate at Paramount's Kings Dominion and Kings Island) built by the Japanese firm. After being secured in cleverly designed supports engineered to adjust to varying heights, riders stand through a 360-degree vertical loop, horizontal helix and tilting sections before re-entering the station.

Below: After exiting the vertical loop, standing Skyriders enter a horizontal spiral, then negotiate some angled track sections.

Above: There's standing room only aboard Skyrider. This TOGO-built coaster enters the vertical loop at speeds of up to 50 miles per hour.

Le MONSTRE

LOCATION: La Ronde, Montreal, Quebec, Canada
YEAR BUILT: 1985
CONSTRUCTOR: William Cobb Associates
MAXIMUM HEIGHT: 131 feet
LENGTH: 3986 and 3994 feet
TOP SPEED: 42 mph
CAPACITY PER TRAIN: 28
LONGEST DROP: 125 feet
RIDE DURATION: 2 minutes 30 seconds
INVERSIONS: 0

Built on the island that originally housed the 1967 Worlds Fair, the massive Le Monstre combines the fun and speed of a twister with the creative engineering of a dual-track coaster. William Cobb's intricate layout allows the tracks to crisscross on twelve different occasions, and riders lucky enough to experience a 'race' with both trains side-by-side are in for a special treat. As one train swoops, climbs and maneuvers through the structure, it disappears from sight, only to appear on the opposite side of train two. The here-and-gone action continues throughout, making rides unique, scenic experiences.

Left: The tracks on Le Monstre crisscross 12 times. Part of the fun of riding is watching the other train appear and disappear.

Below: Montreal's Le Monstre is one of William Cobb's most complex designs and, according to him, his best-engineered coaster.

GOUDURIX

LOCATION: Parc Asterix, Plailly, near Paris, France
YEAR BUILT: 1989
CONSTRUCTOR: Vekoma International
MAXIMUM HEIGHT: 118 feet
LENGTH: 3117 feet
TOP SPEED: 56 mph
CAPACITY PER TRAIN: 28
LONGEST DROP: 108 feet
RIDE DURATION: 2 minutes
INVERSIONS: 7

Below: The Parc Asterix coaster Goudurix offers a variety of elements, including three loops, a double corkscrew, and, at the left of the picture, a boomerang.

With its unique crooked architecture and locally popular cartoon influences, Parc Asterix's quirky atmosphere was perfect for the addition of the entertaining Goudurix in 1989.

A custom-designed seven-inversion thriller by Vekoma International, Goudurix sends riders screaming through three vertical loops, a boomerang element and a corkscrew. The disorienting two-minute trip is highlighted by a 108-foot drop and speeds approaching 56 miles per hour.

Right: Following two loops directly off the first drop, riders now encounter their third and fourth inversions as they enter the boomerang element.

SPACE MOUNTAIN

LOCATION: Disneyland Paris,
  Marne La Vallée, Cedex, France
YEAR BUILT: 1994
CONSTRUCTOR: Vekoma International
MAXIMUM HEIGHT: 105 feet
LENGTH: 3281 feet
TOP SPEED: 44 mph
CAPACITY PER TRAIN: 24
RIDE DURATION: 2 minutes
INVERSIONS: 4

Different from Disney's previous Space Mountain coasters in that it utilizes a catapult-launch system, this newest version also features an ornately designed Jules Verne-inspired outside structure. A trip into space begins with a launch from the Columbiad Cannon into total darkness. The six-car, 24-passenger vehicles are outfitted with digital on-board audio systems, providing music that sets the tone for a fantastic journey including fast turns, sudden drops and four inversions.

Below: The colorfully-themed façade creates a 'Jules Verne' atmosphere on the ride. The building is more than thirteen stories high.

Below: Parts of the Columbiad cannon move and smoke every time a train is launched into Space Mountain at Disneyland Paris.

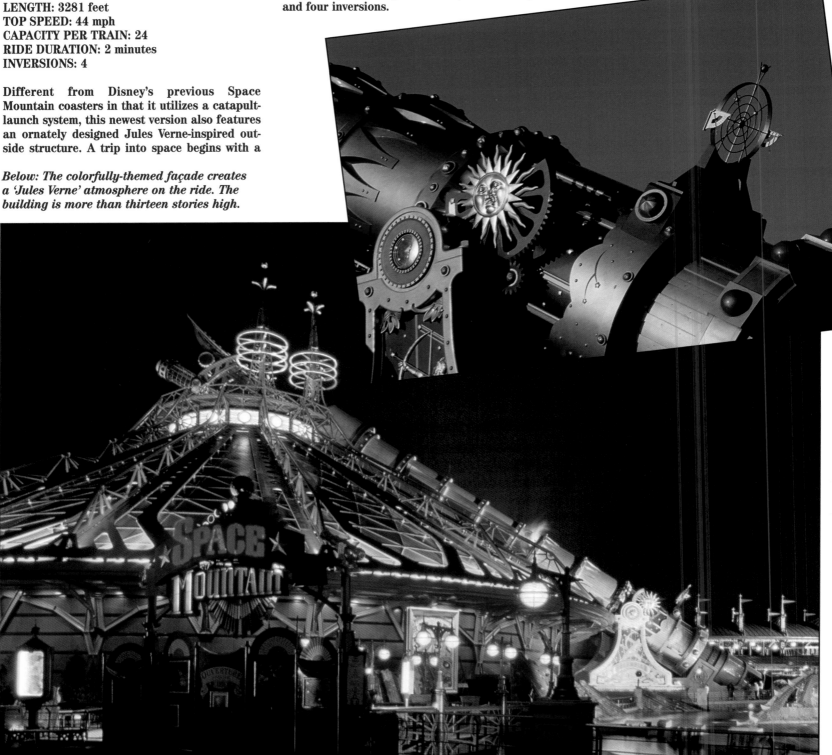

GRAND NATIONAL

LOCATION: Blackpool Pleasure Beach,
 Blackpool, England
YEAR BUILT: 1935
CONSTRUCTOR: Blackpool Pleasure Beach
MAXIMUM HEIGHT: 67 feet
LENGTH: 3302 feet
TOP SPEED: 50 mph
CAPACITY PER TRAIN: 24
LONGEST DROP: 60 feet
RIDE DURATION: 2 minutes 20 seconds
INVERSIONS: 0

*Right: Styled on England's best-loved
steeplechase, Grand National's 'jumps' carry
the names of the fences on the Aintree course.
Seen through the crossbeams of the second
turn, yellow leads blue over Valentine's Brook.*

*Below: Designed by American Charles Paige,
each train travels 12000 miles in a season.*

Blackpool Pleasure Beach occupies 42 acres of
the seafront on Blackpool's South Shore.
Beginning in 1896 with just one ride, the park
now boasts over 145 rides and attractions.

One of four wooden coasters built here in the
1930s, Grand National was 61 years of age in
1996, the park's Centenary year. A twin racer, it
has one Möbius loop of track, returning trains to
the opposite side of the loading station.

*Below: In the home straight the track dips
under a walkway, rising to the winning post
and loading station. Blue wins by a length!*

BLACKPOOL PLEASURE BEACH®
THE BIG ONE HUNDRED
CENTENARY
1896–1996

The PEPSI MAX BIG ONE

LOCATION: Blackpool Pleasure Beach,
  Blackpool, England
YEAR BUILT: 1994
CONSTRUCTOR: Arrow Dynamics
MAXIMUM HEIGHT: 201 feet
LENGTH: 5497 feet
TOP SPEED: 85 mph
CAPACITY PER TRAIN: 30
LONGEST DROP: 205 feet
RIDE DURATION: 2 minutes
INVERSIONS: 0

THE PEPSI MAX BIG ONE

Topped by aircraft warning beacons, The Pepsi Max Big One was Europe's tallest coaster in 1996, towering to the dizzy heights of 235 feet above the South Shore at Blackpool. The £12 million investment was a complex engineering project, since the ride was required to travel over and around several existing rides on the site. Some pilings were driven over 45 feet down through sand to find a solid base. The 2600-tonne steel structure was produced in sections in nearby Bolton, and delivered to Blackpool

Left: The massive steel structure of the Pepsi Max Big One towers above the twinkling seafront lights of Blackpool's South Shore. Photograph by Lord Lichfield.

Above left: Each train begins its mile-long run with a 205-foot, 65 degree angle drop, incorporating a swooping right-hand turn. Photograph by Lord Lichfield.

Airport, the nearest open space to the coaster site. Here some sections were assembled into larger units which were then transported to the seafront. Construction on the site took place between November 1993 and March 1994. The finished ride is protected by no less than five coats of paint. Inside the loading station, trains are stacked vertically on a lift mechanism.

In 1994, its first operational season, the Pepsi Max Big One produced a 25% increase in turnover for Blackpool Pleasure Beach.

The ULTIMATE

LOCATION: Lightwater Valley, North Stainley,
 Ripon, North Yorkshire, England
YEAR BUILT: 1991
CONSTRUCTOR: Big Country Motioneering
MAXIMUM HEIGHT: 107 feet
LENGTH: 7542 feet
TOP SPEED: 60 mph
CAPACITY PER TRAIN: 38
LONGEST DROP: 157 feet
RIDE DURATION: 5 minutes 50 seconds
INVERSIONS: 0

*Left: Accelerating off the first drop, the train
then follows the natural contours of the North
Yorkshire countryside.*

*Below: The run from the crest of the second
lift hill back into the loading station is one
continuous descent, totalling 157 feet.*

In 1996 *The Guinness Book Of Records* listed
The Ultimate as the longest roller coaster in the
world. Designed by park owner Robert Staveley,
construction work began in early 1990 and was
completed over a period of eighteen months,
opening on July 17, 1991.

The £5.2 million ride begins with a 102-foot
lift hill of Canadian Redwood trestles. Its tubular steel track winds through 44 acres of the
175-acre park, rising at the halfway point onto a
second, 107-foot lift hill. Trains take almost six
minutes to complete the circuit.

LIGHTWATER VALLEY
THE ACTION ATTRACTION

NEMESIS

LOCATION: Alton Towers, near Alton, Staffordshire, England
YEAR BUILT: 1994
CONSTRUCTOR: Bolliger & Mabillard
MAXIMUM HEIGHT: 104 feet
LENGTH: 2350 feet
TOP SPEED: 50 mph
CAPACITY PER TRAIN: 32
LONGEST DROP: 43 feet
RIDE DURATION: 1 minute 30 seconds
INVERSIONS: 4

Right: Riders board inside the belly of the alien creature, and are spewed out onto the lift hill in the background.

Left: Located in Forbidden Valley, Nemesis represented a £12 million investment, and became the park's fifth full-size coaster.

Below: Trains depart every 50 seconds, carrying 1400 riders per hour. A total of 7452 bolts were used in the construction.

Alton Towers is a 500-acre park set in the landscaped gardens of a ruined country mansion, and boasts over 125 rides and attractions.

Opened on March 28, 1994, Nemesis became Europe's first suspended looping coaster. Designer John Wardley's creation, fashioned from 440 tons of steel, nestles in the solid rock of a ravine where the alien creature crouches in its underground lair. A pool fills with blood from streams cascading down the rock wall. Riders are afforded an unnerving upside-down view of this as they crest the 360-degree loop, which pulls four Gs on the way in and out.

DRAGON KHAN

LOCATION: Port Aventura, Vila Seca,
  Tarragona, Spain
YEAR BUILT: 1995
CONSTRUCTOR: Bolliger & Mabillard
MAXIMUM HEIGHT: 148 feet
LENGTH: 4165 feet
TOP SPEED: 68 mph
CAPACITY PER TRAIN: 28
LONGEST DROP: 161 feet
RIDE DURATION: 3 minutes
INVERSIONS: 8

Another Bolliger & Mabillard engineering marvel, Dragon Khan delivers an amazing first drop, featuring strong negative Gs. The tangled red and powder blue structure sends riders upside-down a record-setting eight times, smoothly through non-stop elements that include a 118-foot tall vertical loop, a dive loop, 'cobra' roll, zero-G 'heartline' roll, another vertical loop, a high-speed spiral and two interlocked corkscrews. Trains carry 32 passengers in eight rows of four-across seats.

Left: Bolliger & Mabillard broke their previous world record of 108 feet (on Kumba, page 60), with this outrageous 118-foot tall loop.

Above: In 1996, Port Aventura's Dragon Khan held the all-time record for most inversions on a coaster: riders are flipped eight times.

Right: The elements on Spain's Dragon Khan occur in the same order as America's Kumba, with the addition of one extra loop.

BANDIT

LOCATION: Yomiuri Land, Inagi, Tokyo, Japan
YEAR BUILT: 1988
CONSTRUCTOR: TOGO Japan
MAXIMUM HEIGHT: 167 feet
LENGTH: 5117 feet
TOP SPEED: 69 mph
CAPACITY PER TRAIN: 28
RIDE DURATION: 3 minutes 7 seconds
INVERSIONS: 0

The topography of the park combined with the technology of the manufacturer resulted in the Bandit, a custom-designed coaster built by TOGO Japan. It's one of the world's fastest, reaching speeds of nearly 70 miles per hour. Designers took advantage of the hilly terrain to achieve an elevation difference of 256 feet, setting a record upon its installation in 1988. One ride lasts just over three minutes.

Left: Along the course, the Bandit's height difference exceeds 250 feet. The three-minute ride treats riders to speeds nearing 70mph.

Above: Bandit was custom designed by TOGO Japan to fit the topography of Yomiuri Land.

WHITE CANYON

Below: White Canyon's southern yellow pine wood structure was prefabricated in the United States and shipped to the Japanese park.

Bottom: White Canyon is the world's tallest and longest Cyclone-style coaster, utilizing more than one million board feet of lumber.

LOCATION: Yomiuri Land, Inagi, Tokyo, Japan
YEAR BUILT: 1994
CONSTRUCTOR: TOGO Japan/RCCA
MAXIMUM HEIGHT: 115 feet
LENGTH: 3609 feet
TOP SPEED: 52 mph
CAPACITY PER TRAIN: 28
LONGEST DROP: 95 feet
RIDE DURATION: 2 minutes 35 seconds
INVERSIONS: 0

A joint effort by TOGO, the Roller Coaster Corporation of America, John Pierce Associates and Morgan Manufacturing produced the 115-foot tall White Canyon at Yomiuri Land park in Tokyo, Japan in 1994. Wooden coasters are a rarity in Japan, due to strict building codes and regulations prohibiting tall wooden structures.

Chapter Three

WHITE KNUCKLE, WET KNUCKLE

Combine height, speed
and imagined danger and you
have some of the ingredients
for a true thrill ride.
Include darkness, fear, and
the element of surprise
for extra effect.
Then, to complete the
mixture, just add water...

Although there are a vast number of ways to thrill humans safely, one would think that amusement ride manufacturers would have run out of creative ways to accomplish this many years ago. Fortunately, this has not been the case. Many of today's thrill rides have roots dating back to the amusement parks of the early 1900s - especially those at Coney Island, which, in its heyday, became a proving ground of sorts for some of the most innovative and unusual rides of all time. Today, rides like the Whirl-Fly, Human Pool Table and Roulette Wheel are part of amusement history, having been replaced by state-of-the-art high-tech thrillers with names like Chaos, Evolution, Mixer, Play Ball, Space Shot and Top Spin. Rides are manufactured all over the world, giving the parks that install them a truly international flavor. After all, when it comes to screaming, it's clear that there are no language barriers.

Most parks have managed to change with the times and install these new technological wonders while still keeping some of the popular thrillers that preceded them. An exciting blend

Below: This innocent looking and very rare Turbo ride has appeared at the Western Washington State Fair in Puyallup, Washington.

of old and new rides can mean the difference between a good park and a great one. In fact, a developing trend in the mid 1990s has been for some of the more established parks to develop entire sections dedicated to preserving nostalgia, celebrating and sometimes recreating the golden years of classic amusement rides.

During the last 30 years, one of the easiest ways to experience a few minutes of sheer terror has been to climb aboard a diabolical machine called the Turbo. This innocent looking ride consists of small, round seats or 'capsules' which are attached to arms resembling the spokes of a wheel. A Turbo has two of these wheels which rotate independently. The two wheels are attached to a central hub which also rotates. Each capsule can accommodate two riders. The back of the capsules are attached to the spokes with a pivoting coupler that allows free movement af the car in all directions (even some you never knew existed!). The result: when those wheels start to rotate, you'll feel like that little ball in an empty spray paint can. The free-moving capsules can (and will) spin and turn in all directions and you'll soon find yourself being pulled upside down by your head and back, and thrown into every conceivable position. During a ride on the Turbo, you are guaranteed to lose all sense of direction, not to mention everything in your pockets.

According to the manufacturer, there were only 23 Turbos ever made... possibly a blessing in disguise. (Today, most of the remaining Turbo rides can be found in Brazil. At the time of this writing, the only one operating in a permanent park in North America is at Old Indiana Family Fun 'N Waterpark in Thorntown, Indiana). If you're a true whiteknuckler, find one and give it a try. It's an experience you won't soon forget. Two words of advice: Ride alone.

Other disorienting rides of the same genre include the popular Zipper and Loop-O-Plane, which deliver a similar feeling as the Turbo, but mainly in one direction. These two can be found mostly in traveling shows and occasionally at permanent parks.

CATCH A WAVE

Among the new generation of large capacity thrillers is the Waikiki Wave Super Flip, one of which can be found at Mexico City's Reino Aventura theme park (they call it the Hurricane, for good reason). If you have ever seen salt water taffy being made, this ride has the same movements, and you'll feel like the taffy. The Waikiki Wave Super Flip sees 40 riders on a platform (two rows of 20 sitting back to back). The

Right: Rows of guests at Mexico City's Reino Aventura scramble their senses on the popular Hurricane – a Waikiki Wave Super Flip ride.

ride has two rotating arms attached to the ends of the platform. When the arms are parallel, the platform (and occupants) can be flipped over forward and backward at various heights. When the arms are turning independently, the flipping can be combined with diagonal positioning of the platform, producing an assortment of aerial sensations.

With many of the classic amusement devices of the past, many ride operators would pride themselves in being able to 'work the ride' and deliver maximum thrills by knowing just how to operate the controls to their fullest capacity. This element has been largely eliminated with

Left: The Twilight Zone Tower of Terror freefall attraction is housed in the foreboding Hollywood Tower Hotel at the end of Sunset Boulevard, in the Disney-MGM Studios Theme Park, Orlando, Florida.

the computer-controlled rides of today. Now, it is common for rides to have a variety of intensity settings from mild to wild, and the operator or park owner simply chooses which program to run. A bit of the human element has been eliminated, but luckily, park patrons keep screaming for more intense rides, and the manufacturers have been eager to deliver.

STRAIGHT UP, AND STRAIGHT DOWN

In the 1980s, Intamin AG, a Swiss ride manufacturer, decided it might be interesting to confine passengers in a steel cage and drop them off the side of a 13-story building. The Freefall ride was created and does exactly that.

Some consider the Freefall a vertical roller coaster. It consists of a skeletal steel elevator-like tower which transports a four-passenger car to the top. Once there, the car moves to the outside of the tower where it hangs precariously for

Above: Cedar Point's Freefall is called the Demon Drop, where a car containing up to four guests (inset) is dropped off the side of an elevator-like tower.

a second. Then, without warning, the car drops straight down on the outside of the structure guided by small wheels on a track. Toward the bottom of the tower, the track curves away from the tower (picture a large letter 'L'). As the car continues, it becomes horizontal and the passengers inside are now on their backs, looking at the sky. When the ride is over, the car moves onto a lower track, rights itself, and allows the passengers to disembark safely.

There are nearly a dozen Freefall rides operating in the world, with names like the Demon Drop, Texas Cliffhanger and Sky Screamer, all identical. Two are indoors. West Edmonton Mall's glittering Galaxyland park features a

Freefall called The Daring Drop of Doom which allows passengers to catch a brief glimpse of the Edmonton skyline through a window at the top of the ride just before plummeting back into the mall below.

The other indoor Freefall-style ride is a custom-designed installation at the Disney-MGM Studios Theme Park in Orlando, Florida. Most Disney rides have a story behind them and the Tower of Terror is no exception. Legend has it that a freak lightning storm struck The Hollywood Tower Hotel during a party on Halloween night in 1939, mysteriously transporting five elevator passengers to The Twilight Zone. Guests have the opportunity to check in to the hotel and relive that fateful evening. After watching a televised summary of the bizarre Halloween disappearances, the Tower of Terror visitors proceed into the basement of the building to board one of four 'elevators' and relive the event. The core of the whole attraction is essentially four heavily themed Freefalls, featuring some excellent special effects and unusual occurrences along the way.

Above: The innocent looking frontage of the Haunted House at Knoebels Amusement Resort hides an excellent traditional dark ride. Courageous guests are 'welcomed' at the door (right), and led into a maze of dark and sinister corridors.

Intamin has introduced two variations to the Freefall ride, utilizing updated technology. The first, called the Giant Drop, is a pole-type tower with four-passenger cars attached to it. These travel independently up and down the sides. While the ride sensation is basically the same as a Freefall, the Giant Drop has some obvious differences from its predecessor. The big change is in the transport system. Linear induction motors are used to power the cars to the top, doubling as brakes to ease the cars to a stop on the return trip. There's no comforting horizontal braking system this time around... it's straight up and, yes, straight down. The prototype Giant Drop, Kentucky Kingdom's Hellevator, stands more than 160 feet tall. Newer installations, such as the Drop Zone at Paramount's Great America, are more than 200 feet tall.

A larger variation on the Giant Drop is called the Gyro Drop. Instead of individual cars, the Gyro Drop transports passengers in one large circular cabin, holding 40 or more riders. The cabin rotates as it travels up the tower, then upon arrival, quickly drops straight down.

A HAUNTING EXPERIENCE

Most people agree that it's fun to be scared (at least, they say they do). For decades, walk-through and ride-through haunted houses have been a staple in amusement parks, tourist areas and traveling shows worldwide. Unfortunately, in recent years, under tremendous scrutiny by

Right: Der Stuka, at Wet 'n Wild waterpark in Las Vegas, is an exhilarating 76-foot freefall slide. Riders on Blue Niagara, a twisting twin water tube, launch themselves from a lower level of the same structure.

Below: The always inventive Action Park in McAfee, New Jersey, was the first in the world to construct a water slide with a vertical loop.

fire and safety officials and steadily increasing liability insurance costs, many of the great ones have been removed. Others have met their demise to make room for newer attractions, or have been torn down because the traditional parks they were in closed forever. Fortunately, a handful of the best still exist. For a first-class traditional ride-through haunted experience, you won't find any better than the Haunted House at Knoebels Amusement Resort in Pennsylvania. The nondescript façade of the house effectively

Above: Kentucky Kingdom's Mile High Falls shoot-the-chutes attraction is nearly one hundred feet high, creating a considerable splash when the boat reaches the bottom of the ramp.

belies the total sensory overload waiting for unsuspecting visitors inside. One or two brave explorers can ride in the classic highbacked cars and travel through a seemingly endless labyrinth of creepy crawlers, gravesites, noises and confusion in the darkness. This is one ride you have to experience a few times just to make sure you didn't miss something the first time around (you did). When you go back for an encore performance, sit on the opposite side of the car to get the full impact.

A similar attraction can be found at Funland Amusement Park on the boardwalk in Rehoboth Beach, Delaware. The Haunted Mansion, constructed in 1979, is a two-story traditional haunted house wlth a modern (and rare) twist: the cars are suspended from an overhead track. To add to the spooky effect, the park only operates the ride at night. The rides at Knoebels and Funland remain entertaining and popular sea-

Left: Only a few seconds from splashdown... After meandering through the winding course, log flumes like this example at Knoebels Amusement Resort in Elysburg, Pennsylvania, cap off the journey with an exciting finale.

son after season, because of the commitment by the owners to keep the 'stunts' inside operating in top condition.

Disney's Haunted Mansions (Florida and California) and Phantom Manor (Paris) are more modern versions of the classic ride-through haunted house and are extremely well designed. During your trip through the dark hallways, you'll interact with ghosts and goblins of every description and may even find a stowaway in the car with you! Be sure to read the entertaining inscriptions on the grave markers outside.

There are several walk-through haunted dwellings that give a whole new dimension to the phrase 'This Old House'. A few that are worth driving out of your way to visit include Dr. Frankenstein's Castle at Indiana Beach, the Haunted House at Oregon's Enchanted Forest, the Casona del Terror at Mexico City's La Feria, and the Passaje del Terror at Reino Aventura (an upcharge from the Pay-One-Price admission, but well worth it). Every October, Universal Studios Florida transforms several of its sound-stages into monster-filled walk-throughs with names like the Psycho Path and Terror Underground. Although only temporary (usually featured for 10 to 15 days during the park's Halloween event), these attractions utilize props from the famous Universal horror films and rate among the very best of their kind.

MAKING A SPLASH

Since their inception, amusement and theme parks have used water as one of their main ingredients in their recipes for fun. Sooner or later everyone queues up for a ride that includes the bonus of a cool splash of water on a hot summer afternoon, and manufacturers continue to design creative ways to safely deliver both for parks and their guests.

While entrepreneur George Millay was building the Sea World marine life park in the hot, muggy climate of Orlando, Florida, he began to formulate an idea for a new type of theme park – a facility that would attract locals and tourists alike to don their swimsuits and enjoy an assortment of water-related activities and attractions or just relax and bask in the Florida sun. In 1974, Millay formed Wet 'n Wild Inc. to study the feasibility of creating a totally water-oriented theme park and, in 1977, the world's first full themed waterpark – Wet 'n Wild – opened in Orlando. Success was immediate. Although nearby Walt Disney World had already opened a water activity area called River Country, Wet 'n Wild featured a wave pool and many other elements that have become standards in the waterpark industry. Today, there are hundreds of waterparks worldwide, indoors and outdoors, in malls, on rooftops and increasingly as part of existing amusement and theme parks.

Above: Another party of adventurers makes its escape! On the partially enclosed shoot-the-chutes ride Escape From Pompeii at Busch Gardens Williamsburg, Williamsburg, Virginia, boats filled with visiting 'explorers' come face to face with the burning ruins of Pompeii, before thundering out onto the drop ramp for a refreshing splashdown.

at Busch Gardens

the tubes propelled by more than 1000 gallons of water per minute. The tubes are enhanced with special effects, sounds, lighting and fog.

For sheer numbers of slides, nothing tops the tangled Super Whopper complex in Kobe Harbor, Japan, which features 50 separate water slides (the longest one measures 500 feet long) on one structure, adding up to more than four miles of chutes.

An array of unusual water attractions can be enjoyed at Action Park in McAfee, New Jersey. With a long track record of introducing creative one-of-a-kind rides, it was logical that Action Park would be the park to introduce the Tube Loop – the world's first tube water slide with a vertical loop.

Even with all the advances in technology, one common property of water is that it doesn't flow uphill... at least, it *didn't*, until the amusement park industry got hold of it. In 1991, attorney-turned-inventor Tom Lochtefeld introduced his patented system of 'water injection technology' – a series of small nozzles that shoot a very thin, powerful and controllable 'sheet' of water onto a surface (even uphill), instantly forming the basis for a new generation of exciting water rides. Teaming up with Jeff Henry at Water Ride Concepts, Lochtefeld's new invention was first

As demand for the waterparks grew in the late 1970s and early 1980s, a new breed of ride manufacturers began to surface, offering unique ways to transport swimmers through tubes, down slides, out of troughs and into pools. Concrete spillways soon evolved into fiberglass, and odd-looking tubular structures began to take shape at waterparks everywhere. As with roller coasters, there seems to be no end to the different ways to get the same results... in this case, thrilled *and* wet. Once again, a Disney park has created a superlative attraction – the 120-foot tall Summit Plummet at Florida's Blizzard Beach is the tallest and fastest water speed slide in the world, sending its guests careening down a 65 degree incline at speeds approaching 55 miles per hour. Steep slides like Wet 'n Wild's Der Stuka and Geronimo provide similar terror.

Another thrilling invention unique to the Wet 'n Wild parks is the Bomb Bay: a bomb-shaped enclosure large enough for guests to stand inside – but not long enough to get comfortable. Once the passenger is secure inside, the 'bomb' is positioned over a slide. The 'floor' opens, and the rider plummets feet-first 70 feet straight down toward a splash pool at the bottom.

In 1990, Wet 'n Wild debuted The Black Hole, a $2 million cosmic-themed structure supporting two 500-foot long enclosed black tubes and topped with a 66-foot saucer-shaped 'space-ship'. Passengers ride inflatable 'jet sleds' down

Above: Disney's Splash Mountain attractions are the longest and most elaborate log flumes in the world. Riders experience the 'Song of the South' in a spectacular animatronic riverboat scene inside the 'mountain'.

Below: River rapids rides offer a different ride every time and are lots of fun on a hot day. Paramount's Kings Dominion's White Water Canyon is one of the absolute wettest, twisting through geysers, rapids and waterfalls.

utilized in a ride called the Flow Rider, a water attraction that replicates a 'perfect' surfing wave. The first Flow Rider installed at a park was Boogie Bahn, at Schlitterbahn in San Antonio, Texas. The Flow Rider wave machine makes a curl so perfect, it has been used for international surfing competitions.

In 1992, Water Ride Concepts again used water injection technology to build a Drag Race, where raft riders could square off against each other by blasting down fiberglass tracks powered only by water. But the biggest technological advance in waterparks in the first half of the decade was the Master Blaster, first tested in 1993. Employing a 'vertical linear accelerator' that could power riders uphill, a 25-foot tall Master Blaster Uphill Water Coaster opened at Schlitterbahn in summer 1994.

Log flumes and shoot-the-chutes have been favorites at the parks for decades. Tokyo Disneyland's Splash Mountain flume can accommodate 62 boats and is the tallest and longest, at more than 70 feet high and 2788 feet long. Shoot-the-chutes are variations on the flume ride, with a shorter course, larger boats, and a bigger splash. Be prepared to get completely soaked on the tallest ones, which include Hersheypark's Tidal Force, Kentucky Kingdom's Mile High

Below: Award-winning producer Douglas Trumbull developed the special film format for Back to the Future – The Ride at the Universal Studios Theme Parks, a very convincing simulator experience.

Above: Raging Rapids in Boulder Canyon at Indiana's Holiday World is an example of an eight-passenger river rapids ride with the added attraction of western theming along the course.

Falls, Dorney Park's White Water Landing, and Cedar Point's Snake River Falls.

In 1980, Houston's AstroWorld theme park debuted a new concept in amusement rides: a 'river rapids' ride called Thunder River. Large, round raft-boats float freely through a winding course, rebounding off the banks as they pass under waterfalls and near geysers. As with flumes, getting soaked is the main attraction here, but the added feature of the spinning, uncontrollable rafts makes the ride exciting. No two trips through the rapids are ever the same.

FLIGHTS OF IMAGINATION

While not technically a ride, a simulator attraction appeals to theme parks because it can be operated in any kind of weather, attracts a large range of age groups, and the theme can be easily changed after a period of time. Thanks to major advances in computers and motion base technology, simulators can now recreate the feeling of riding or flying. Back To The Future – The Ride, at Universal Studios in Florida and California, allows guests to experience a frenzied chase through time, just as in the movie.

What's on the horizon for thrill rides in the 21st century? Imagination is the only limit. Parks and manufacturers are continuously introducing new ways to appeal to every fantastic wish of guests around the world. If you dream of excitement, sooner or later you'll be able to experience it your way in an amusement park.

Chapter Four

THE PARKS LISTING

These are the addresses, contact telephone numbers, opening times and more, of all the amusement parks featured in this volume.

One of the many unique aspects of amusement and theme parks is that everyone can enjoy the attractions at their own pace and in any order they choose. Before you leave for the park, think about what you will be doing once you arrive and plan accordingly. You'll find that a few minutes of planning can make your day much more enjoyable and save you considerable money as well. Since parks are usually somewhat isolated from the rest of the world, whatever you don't bring, you'll most likely have to buy. Think about film, strollers, sunscreen and other medications, extra clothing, and so on.

Much of your time will most likely be spent outdoors and on your feet, so you may want to call ahead to check the weather forecast – especially if the park you are traveling to is a long distance away. Remember to dress for the *entire* day's weather and wear comfortable clothes and shoes. Bring along extra clothes if the nights are cooler... you can rent a locker inside the park or leave the clothes in your car (most parks will allow guests to leave and return to the park as long as they have their hand stamped at the gate). Don't forget your swimwear if you plan to spend time in the waterpark. Other than sunscreen and maybe a camera, don't bring a lot of things into the park that you'll have to carry around all day. Most parks won't let you take loose objects on the rides anyway, so leave them in your car.

Another reason to call the park before you visit is to ask if they are offering any discounts or specials the day you plan to go. Many parks discount admission prices when guests present a coupon, ticket or proof-of-purchase from local businesses. Find out what the current promotions are and take advantage of the discounts. You may also want to ask if there are any special events scheduled on the day you plan to visit. For example, a popular performer might be appearing and might encourage you to go on a specific date or cause you to postpone your visit to a less crowded day. Also check to see if admission tickets are sold in places other than the park's front gate. Parks sometimes sell tickets through stores, hotels, and other businesses, saving you from standing in a long line at the entrance.

Generally, parks are less crowded on weekdays and almost always very crowded on the weekends. The earlier or later in the season you can go, the better, but do check opening times with the park. Those quoted in this listing are peak times; park hours can vary considerably in early or late season, and some parks open only on weekends at this time.

The more perfect the weather, the bigger the crowds. Arrive early... you'll find the park becomes the most crowded during the early-to-mid afternoon. Remember where you park your car (write it down!). You won't want to explore a huge dark parking lot at the end of your day.

A general rule of thumb is to obtain a guidebook and/or map of the park. In addition to showing you where everything is, the guidebook will list all the showtimes and special events for that day. Brochures and maps can be found at the Guest Services window. Directional signs and maps are located throughout most parks.

Once inside, do the opposite of what the masses are doing. For example: eat lunch before noon or after 2.30 pm and you will avoid long lines. Remember that most people want to ride the biggest and newest attractions first, so the lines will be longest at those. Browse through the souvenir shops as you go but save your actual buying until you're ready to leave (unless you have rented a locker). That way you won't have to carry bags around with you all day. Decide on a place to meet if you become separated from the rest of your group.

Read and follow the safety rules. Parks are extremely safety-conscious, and it is imperative that you abide by these rules. If you have children, make sure they understand and follow the instructions of the operator.

Above all, have a great time! Parks are excellent places to relax and enjoy a carefree day with friends and family.

The information which follows was accurate at the time of publication, but hours and ride availability are subject to change and can be affected by weather and crowds. Most parks offer reductions in the adult admission price for children and seniors, and very young children are usually admitted free of charge. Call ahead to verify.

ACTION PARK
Route 94
McAfee, New Jersey 07428, USA
(201) 827-2000
A ski resort in the winter, this unusual and exciting park is packed with dozens of 'guest-powered' attractions, water rides, go-kart tracks and much more.
Season: Late May – early September
Hours: 10 am – 9 pm
Admission: Pay-One-Price
Parking: Free

ADVENTURELAND PARK
I-80 and Highway 65
Des Moines, Iowa 50316-0355, USA
(515) 266-2121
This well-landscaped park features replicas of historic Iowa buildings and a variety of standard thrill rides, two great wooden coasters, OUTLAW and TORNADO, and a double-looping steel coaster called the DRAGON.
Season: Late April – September

Hours: 10am – 10pm
Admission: Pay-One-Price
Parking: Daily charge

ADVENTURE WORLD
13710 Central Avenue
Largo, Maryland 20775-4210, USA
(301) 249-1500
Located just outside Washington, DC, Adventure World is half waterpark and half amusement park. The amusement park side contains the speedy WILD ONE woodie, the suspended looping MIND ERASER, the PYTHON shuttle loop, and Iron Eagle, a rare Rotoshake ride.
Season: Early May – October
Hours: 10 am – 9 pm
Admission: Pay-One-Price
Parking: Daily charge

ALTON TOWERS
Staffordshire ST10 4DB
England
(01538) 702200
The UK's largest theme park boasts Europe's first inverted looping coaster, NEMESIS, alongside over 120 other rides and attractions in 500 acres of landscaped gardens.
Season: March – November
Hours: 9 am opening. (Rides open 10 am)
Closing time varies according to time of season
Admission: Pay-One-Price
Parking: Free

ASTROLAND AMUSEMENT PARK
1000 Surf Avenue
Brooklyn, New York 11224-2800, USA

(718) 265-2100
Built on the most famous amusement property in the world, Astroland offers a midway of thrillers and the classic CYCLONE.
Season: April – September
Hours: Noon – Midnight
Admission: Free: Pay-One-Price or individual ride tickets
Parking: Various (Aquarium lot next door is recommended)

BELMONT PARK
3190 Mission Blvd.
San Diego, California 92109, USA
(619) 488-1549
The classic seaside GIANT DIPPER coaster is the focus of this amusement center, surrounded by shops, a few rides and other attractions.
Season: Year-round
Hours: 11 am – 10 pm (summer)
Admission: Free: individual ride tickets
Parking: Various

BLACKPOOL PLEASURE BEACH
Ocean Boulevard, Blackpool FY4 1EZ
England
(01253) 341033
No park has a greater concentration of attractions; squeezed into just 42 acres are rides old and new, including the giant coaster THE PEPSI MAX BIG ONE, pictured below.
Season: March – November
Hours: 10 am opening
Closing time varies according to time of season
Pay-As-You-Ride
Parking: South Shore car parks (pay-per-hour)

BUFFALO BILL'S RESORT CASINO
Route I-15 at NV/CA State Line
Primadonna, Nevada 89109, USA
(702) 382-1111
The first casino to install a world class roller coaster, Buffalo Bill's is the home of the record-setting DESPERADO, Adventure Canyon log flume, train ride, motion simulator and more.
Season: Year-round
Hours: 10 am – 10 pm (attractions)
Admission: Free: individual ride tickets
Parking: Free

BUSCH GARDENS TAMPA BAY
3000 Busch Blvd.
Tampa, Florida 33674-9158, USA
(813) 987-5000
A beautiful 300-acre African-themed park containing more than 3,400 animals along with the KUMBA and MONTU coasters, thrill rides, live entertainment, shops, and restaurants.
Season: Year-round
Hours: 9:30 am – 6 pm
(extended during summer and holidays)
Admission: Pay-One-Price
Parking: Daily charge

BUSCH GARDENS WILLIAMSBURG
One Busch Gardens Blvd.
Williamsburg, Virginia 23187-8785
USA
(804) 253-3350
Three top-notch steel coasters and more than 30 other rides are located in this immaculate park, Virginia's top visitor attraction. Authentically themed to medieval Europe, nine detailed 17th-century hamlets nestle among the rolling, wooded hills.
Season: Late March – October
Hours: 10 am – 10 pm
Admission: Pay-One-Price
Parking: Daily charge

CANOBIE LAKE PARK
North Policy Street
Salem, New Hampshire 03079-0190, USA
(603) 893-3506
The wooded lakeside setting makes for perfect surroundings at this popular traditional New England park. There are dozens of exciting rides and attractions, including the always peppy YANKEE CANNONBALL wooden coaster.
Season: April – September.
Hours: Noon – 10 pm
Admission: Pay-One-Price
Parking: Free

Left: Early evening on the South Shore... The Pepsi Max Big One towers above the floodlit frontage of Blackpool Pleasure Beach, Lancashire, England.

CEDAR POINT
Sandusky, Ohio 44871-8006, USA
(419) 626-0830
For thrill-seekers, this park is nirvana.
Continuing to hold world records for most
coasters and most rides in a single park, Cedar
Point's big selection of thrillers include the
MANTIS, RAPTOR, MEAN STREAK and
MAGNUM XL-200.
Season: Early May – September
Hours: 9 am — 10 pm or midnight
Admission: Pay-One-Price
Parking: Daily charge

CHESSINGTON WORLD OF ADVENTURES
Chessington, Surrey KT9 2NE,
England
(01372) 727227
Europe's first suspended coaster, the VAMPIRE,
can be found here, not to mention the exciting
adventure ride TERRORTOMB, and the
formidable RAMESES REVENGE.
Season: March – November
Hours: 10am – 5 or 6 pm
(10 am – 9.30 pm during late July and August)
Admission: Pay-One-Price
Parking: Free

CLEMENTON AMUSEMENT PARK & SPLASH WORLD
144 Berlin Road
Clementon, New Jersey 08021-0132, USA
(609) 783-0263
Featuring the oldest operating wooden coaster
in the world still in its original location (the
JACK RABBIT), traditional Clementon Park
offers a variety of adult and children's rides,
games, petting zoo and waterpark.
Season: Mid-May – early September
Hours: Noon – 10 pm
Admission: Pay-One-Price
Parking: Free

DISNEYLAND
1313 Harbor Blvd.
Anaheim, California 92803-3232, USA
(714) 999-4000
The theme park that revolutionized an industry
remains one of the world's greatest parks
today. Attractions like the Haunted Mansion,
Splash Mountain, Indiana Jones Adventure and
SPACE MOUNTAIN are among the many
highlights of this outstanding facility.
Season: Year-round
Hours: 9 am – midnight or 1 am
(less during winter months)
Admission: Pay-One-Price
Parking: Daily charge

DISNEYLAND PARIS
Marne La Vallée

Cedex 4 77777 France
(33) 164744371
Many of the popular attractions from the other
Disney theme parks have been incorporated
into this relative newcomer, which many
consider to be the most beautiful Disney park
yet. Phantom Manor, SPACE MOUNTAIN and
BIG THUNDER MOUNTAIN are among the
favorites here.
Season: Year-round
Hours: 10 am – 10 pm
Admission: Pay-One-Price

DORNEY PARK & WILDWATER KINGDOM
3830 Dorney Park Road
Allentown, Pennsylvania 18104-5899, USA
(610) 395-3724
This century-old traditional park features an
assortment of modern thrill rides, the hillside
HERCULES and classic THUNDERHAWK
wooden coasters, a popular waterpark and
many other attractions.
Season: May – September
Hours: 10 am – 10 pm
Admission: Pay-One-Price
Parking: Daily charge

ELITCH GARDENS
I-25 & Speer Blvd.
Denver, Colorado 80202, USA
(303) 455-4771
After more than 100 years at its original
location, Elitch Gardens moved its entire
operation to a roomier downtown site in 1995,
featuring more than 23 rides, including an
updated version of the famous TWISTER
coaster and an innovative river rapids ride.
Season: May – September
Hours: 10 am – 11 pm
Admission: Pay-One-Price
Parking: Daily charge

FIESTA TEXAS
Loop 1604 & I-10
San Antonio, Texas 78269-0290, USA
210-697-5000
Created in a former quarry, Fiesta Texas
showcases the many facets of the state's
heritage. The 200-acre facility offers excellent
food, shopping, rides, water attractions and
features the world's tallest wooden coaster, the
RATTLER.
Season: Mid-March – December
Hours: 10 am – 10 pm
Admission: Pay-One-Price
Parking: Daily charge

GALAXYLAND (in West Edmonton Mall)
8770 170th Street
Edmonton, Alberta, Canada T5T 4M2
(800) 661-8890

The largest indoor amusement park in North
America is located inside the largest mall in
the world... both are spectacular. In addition
to guaranteed perfect weather, Galaxyland's
many attractions include the triple-looping
MINDBENDER and Daring Drop of Doom
Freefall.
Season: Year-round
Hours: 10 am – 10 pm
Admission: Pay-One-Price
Parking: Free

GRAND SLAM CANYON (at Circus Circus)
2880 Las Vegas Blvd. South
Las Vegas, Nevada 89109, USA
(702) 794-3703
The CANYON BLASTER coaster and Rim
Runner shoot-the-chute ride are among the
attractions in the 300,000-square foot
reflective pink glass "adventuredome" behind
the Circus Circus Casino-Hotel complex in Las
Vegas.
Season: Year-round
Hours: 10 am – 10 pm or midnight
Admission: Pay-One-Price
Parking: Free

THE GREAT ESCAPE
Route 9
Lake George, New York 12845, USA
(518) 792-3500
Fairy tales are the dominant theme of this
Adirondack Mountain fantasy land which
became the new home of the legendary Crystal
Beach COMET roller coaster in 1994.
Season: Late May – early September
Hours: 9:30 am – 6 pm
Admission: Pay-One-Price
Parking: Free

HERSHEYPARK
100 West Hersheypark Drive
Hershey, Pennsylvania 17033-2797, USA
(717) 534-3900
Attractions to satisfy all ages at "The
Sweetest Park on Earth" include the COMET,
SIDEWINDER, SOOPERDOOPERLOOPER,
TRAIL BLAZER, and twisted WILDCAT
coasters along with the record-setting Tidal
Force shoot-the-chute ride.
Season: May – September
Hours: 10 am – 10 pm
Admission: Pay-One-Price
Parking: Daily charge

HOLIDAY WORLD & SPLASHIN' SAFARI
Routes 62 & 245
Santa Claus, Indiana 47579-0179, USA
(812) 937-4401
A family park themed to various holidays is the
setting for one of the world's most exciting

wooden coasters: the RAVEN. Hidden in the woods of the Halloween section, it is bordered by sections celebrating Christmas and Fourth of July, and the Splashin' Safari waterpark.
Season: May – September
Hours: 10 am – 8 pm or 10 pm
Admission: Pay-One-Price
Parking: Free

INDIANA BEACH
306 Indiana Beach Drive
Monticello, Indiana 47960-1299, USA
(219) 583-4141
A 20-acre traditional amusement center, boardwalk and waterpark along a picturesque beach and lakeside setting form the surroundings for the speedy HOOSIER HURRICANE coaster, built partially over the 1,400-acre Lake Shafer.
Season: May – September
Hours: 11 am – 11 pm
Admission: Individual ride tickets
Parking: Free

KENNYWOOD PARK
4800 Kennywood Blvd.
West Mifflin, Pennsylvania 15122-2399, USA
(412) 461-0500
Kennywood is one of the world's most treasured traditional amusement parks and has been granted National Historic Landmark status. The friendly, hometown atmosphere combines with dozens of thrilling rides, four excellent roller coasters and the Lost Kennywood section recalling the amusement parks of the past.
Season: May – September
Hours: Noon – 11 pm
Admission: Pay-One-Price
Parking: Free

KENTUCKY KINGDOM
937 Phillips Lane (Kentucky State Fairgrounds)
Louisville, Kentucky 40209-9287, USA
(502) 366-2231
Here's a colorful entertainment complex that's nicknamed "The Thrill Park" for good reason. Tropically themed Hurricane Bay waterpark is surrounded by a fast-growing amusement section which includes TERROR TO THE SECOND POWER – a suspended looping coaster, three other roller coasters, one of the world's tallest shoot-the-chutes rides, and an assortment of other thrillers.
Season: Early April – October
Hours: 11 am – 10 pm
Admission: Pay-One-Price
Parking: Daily charge

KNOEBELS AMUSEMENT RESORT
Route 487
Elysburg, Pennsylvania 17824-0317, USA

(717) 672-2572
Set in a pine and hardwood forest, this popular family-run traditional park offers a perfect mix of classic and new rides. A 750,000-gallon swimming pool, games, delicious food and dozens of other attractions add up to a great park destination for the entire family.
Season: April – mid-September, December
Hours: 11 am – 10 pm
Admission: Free: individual ride tickets or Pay-One-Price
Parking: Free

KNOTT'S BERRY FARM
8039 Beach Blvd.
Buena Park, California 90620-3225, USA
(714) 827-1776
One of America's original theme parks, Knott's Berry Farm has evolved into a contemporary entertainment center while remaining a very original attraction. The 150-acre facility includes the unique SOAP BOX DERBY RACERS, the Calico Log Ride – a classic themed flume ride, MONTEZOOMA'S REVENGE shuttle loop, JAGUAR! and BOOMERANG coasters.
Season: Year-round
Hours: 10 am – midnight (closes earlier during off-peak months)
Admission: Pay-One-Price
Parking: Daily charge

LA FERIA CHAPULTEPEC MAGICO
Juegos Mecanicos
2 Da. Seccion de Chapultepec
Mexico City, D.F. 11580 Mexico
(52) 52302121
Dozens of rides are packed into this 15-acre amusement park located in the heart of Mexico City, dwarfed by the sprawling, twin-tracked SERPENT OF FIRE wooden coaster.
Season: Year-round
Hours: 10 am – 10 pm
Admission: Nominal entry charge plus individual ride tickets
Parking: Free

LAKEMONT PARK
Routes 36 & 220
Altoona, Pennsylvania 16603, USA
(814) 949-7275
Dating back to 1902, Lakemont is the site of LEAP THE DIPS, the world's oldest roller coaster. Although not operational at publication time, plans are well underway to renovate the historic ride and have it back in operation very soon.
Season: May – early September
Hours: Noon – 9 pm
Admission: Pay-One Price
Parking: Free

LA RONDE
Ile Saint-Hélène
Montreal, Quebec, Canada H3C 1A9
(514) 872-6120
A park created after the close of the 1967 Worlds Fair, picturesque La Ronde is located on an island in the St. Lawrence River and includes LE BOOMERANG, LE MONSTRE and COBRA coasters.
Season: May – September
Hours: 11 am – 1 am
Admission: Pay-One-Price
Parking: Daily charge

LIBERTYLAND
940 Early Maxwell Blvd.
(Mid-South Fairgrounds)
Memphis, Tennessee 38104-5931, USA
(901) 274-8800
Libertyland has an All-American theme, complete with replicas of the Liberty Bell and Independence Hall. It's also the home of an authentic piece of history: ZIPPIN PIPPIN – the oldest operating coaster in North America, which moved to its present site in 1923.
Season: Mid-June – September
Hours: 10 am – 9 pm
Admission: Pay-One-Price
Parking: Free

LIGHTWATER VALLEY COUNTRY THEME PARK
North Stainley, Ripon,
North Yorkshire HG4 3HT, England
(01765) 635321
This beautifully scenic 175-acre country park is home to the world's longest roller coaster, the ULTIMATE.
Season: March – October
Hours: 10am – 5pm
(10am – 6.30pm in high season)
Admission: Pay-One-Price
Parking: Free

MARINELAND
7657 Portage Road
Niagara Falls, Ontario, Canada L2E 6X8
(416) 356-8250
Mainly a marine life park with the added attraction of several rides. One of those is the 5,500-foot long DRAGON MOUNTAIN, among the longest steel roller coasters in the world.
Season: Year-round
(rides operated during summer months)
Hours: 10 am – 9 pm
Admission: Pay-One-Price
Parking: Free

MOREY'S PIER
25th & Boardwalk
North Wildwood, New Jersey 08260, USA

(609) 522-5477
One of the most dynamic amusement piers in the United States, Morey's Pier is jammed with dozens of rides, including the twisting Zoom Phloom, the GREAT NOR'EASTER suspended-looping coaster, and a complete waterpark.
Season: Mid-April – September
Hours: Noon – closing
Admission: Free: Pay-One-Price
Parking: Various

OLD INDIANA FAMILY FUN 'N WATERPARK
Route 47
Thorntown, Indiana 46071-9351, USA
(317) 436-2401
A cozy traditional family park, with an equal mix of rides and attractions for young and old. Of special note is the Turbo ride, one of the few to be found in a permanent amusement park.
Season: Mid-May – September
Hours: 10 am – 8 pm
Admission: Pay-One-Price
Parking: Free

PARAMOUNT CANADA'S WONDERLAND
9580 Jane Street
Vaughan, Ontario, Canada L6A 1S6
(905) 832-7000
One of the most beautifully landscaped theme parks in the world, Canada's Wonderland has the most roller coasters of any single park in Canada, and enough other rides, attractions, shows and events to fill an entire day.
Season: May – September
Hours: 10 am – 10 pm
Admission: Pay-One-Price
Parking: Daily charge

PARAMOUNT'S CAROWINDS
Carowinds Blvd.
Charlotte, North Carolina 28241-0289, USA
(704) 588-2606
The state line between North and South Carolina runs right through Carowinds, along with several exciting rides like the HURLER and THUNDER ROAD woodies and the VORTEX steel standing coaster.
Season: March – September
Hours: 10 am – 10 pm
Admission: Pay-One-Price
Parking: Daily charge

PARAMOUNT'S KINGS DOMINION
I-95
Doswell, Virginia 23047-9988, USA
(804) 876-5000
The GRIZZLY, HURLER, SCOOBY DOO and REBEL YELL combine to make Kings Dominion the only theme park in North America with four wooden coasters. With a variety of steel coasters and other great thrill rides, the 400-acre facility has a total of eight themed areas and a waterpark.
Season: April – early October
Hours: 10 or 10:30 am – 10 pm
Admission: Pay-One-Price
Parking: Daily charge

PARAMOUNT'S KINGS ISLAND
I-71
Kings Island, Ohio 45034, USA
(513) 573-5800
The 350-acre flagship park of the Paramount Parks chain is the home of the longest wooden roller coaster in the world: THE BEAST, plus VORTEX, TOP GUN and a host of other spectacular rides, restaurants, entertainment and WaterWorks waterpark.
Season: April – October
Hours: 9 am – Closing
Admission: Pay-One-Price
Parking: Daily charge

PARC ASTERIX
Plailly 60128
France
(33) 44623131
Parc Asterix offers guests a three-dimensional journey into the world of Asterix, a popular French cartoon character. Unusual architecture, re-creations of French landmarks and exciting rides like the GOUDURIX multi-looping coaster can be found throughout the theme park.
Season: April – October
Hours: 10 – 9 pm
Admission: Pay-One-Price
Parking: Free

PLAYLAND
Exhibition Park
Vancouver, British Columbia, Canada V5K 4W3
(604) 255-5161
Every summer, this traditional amusement park becomes part of the midway for the Pacific National Exhibition. The signature ride is the ROLLER COASTER, a classic wooden twister with an unconventional track layout.
Season: April – September
Hours: 10 am – 10 pm
Admission: Pay-One-Price
Parking: Daily charge

PORT AVENTURA
Highway A-7
Vila-Seca, Tarragona 43480 Spain
(34) 77779033
Five themed worlds filled with exciting rides, shows and other attractions await visitors to Port Aventura. The giant red DRAGON KHAN, located in the China section of the park, is one of Europe's largest and most thrilling steel coasters.

Season: May – October
Hours: 10 am – 8 pm or midnight
Admission: Pay-One-Price
Parking: Free

REINO AVENTURA
Carretara Picacho al Ajusco
Mexico City 14200, Mexico
(52) 56453335
Mexico City's theme park is best known internationally as the former home of Keiko – the killer whale featured in the "Free Willy" movie. This colorful park has many attractions and is still the home of the first Boomerang coaster and a Waikiki Wave Super Flip ride dubbed the Hurricane.
Season: Year-round
Hours: 10 am – 10 pm
Admission: Pay-One-Price or individual ride tickets
Parking: Free

RIVERSIDE PARK
1623 Main Street, Route 159
Agawam, Massachusetts 01001-0307, USA
(413) 786-9300
New England's largest traditional amusement park is Riverside – a regional favorite for more than half a century. Riverside began to attract a national audience in 1983 by installing the unpredictable CYCLONE, a wild wooden twister. The park also features the THUNDERBOLT woodie and dozens of other rides.
Season: April – September
Hours: 11 am – 10 pm
Admission: Pay-One-Price
Parking: Daily charge

SANTA CRUZ BEACH BOARDWALK
400 Beach Street
Santa Cruz, California 95060-5416, USA
(408) 423-5590
The Pacific coast's premier amusement boardwalk sizzles all year round with two thrilling coasters including the GIANT DIPPER, and an assortment of rides, games and food. There's no charge for admission or the spectacular view of the ocean and beach.
Season: Year-round
(weekends during off-peak season)
Hours: 11 am – Closing
Admission: Free: Pay-One-Price
Parking: Various

SIX FLAGS ASTROWORLD
9001 Kirby Drive (off Loop 610)
Houston, Texas 77054-2599, USA
(713) 799-1234
The GREEZED LIGHTNIN' shuttle loop is one of nine different roller coasters operating at AstroWorld, a theme park/waterpark complex

located next to the famed Astrodome. The lushly landscaped facility comprises seven themed lands filled with rides and shows.
Season: March – December
Hours: 10 am – Closing
Admission: Pay-One-Price
Parking: Daily charge

SIX FLAGS CALIFORNIA
26101 Magic Mountain Parkway
Valencia, California 91385-0550, USA
(805) 255-4100
A coaster lover's paradise! SUPERMAN THE ESCAPE, BATMAN THE RIDE, VIPER and NINJA are just a few of the white knuckle thrillers located at this popular theme park/waterpark combination.
Season: Year-round
(daily during summer months)
Hours: 10 am – Closing
Admission: Pay-One-Price
Parking: Daily charge

SIX FLAGS GREAT AMERICA
I-94 at Route 132 (Grand Ave.)
Gurnee, Illinois 60031, USA
(708) 249-1776
One of the largest parks in the midwest, the 300-acre Great America complex offers a varied menu of exciting roller coasters and thrill rides. Tops on the list in the thrill department are the wooden VIPER, and BATMAN THE RIDE and SHOCKWAVE steel coasters.
Season: Late April – September
Hours: 10 am – Closing
Admission: Pay-One-Price
Parking: Daily charge

SIX FLAGS OVER GEORGIA
I-20 & Six Flags Parkway
Atlanta, Georgia 30378-5401, USA
(404) 948-9290
Hilly terrain and colorful landscaping form the backdrop for this 330-acre Dixie jewel. Thrill rides like the Freefall, GEORGIA CYCLONE, MIND BENDER and GREAT AMERICAN SCREAM MACHINE have quickly become guests' favorites. A full selection of other rides complements the coasters.
Season: March – October
Hours: 10 am – Closing
Admission: Pay-One-Price
Parking: Daily charge

SIX FLAGS OVER MID-AMERICA
I-44
Eureka, Missouri 63025-0060, USA
(314) 938-5300
BATMAN THE RIDE and the SCREAMIN' EAGLE lead the list of exciting coasters and other attractions at this Six Flags Theme Park just southwest of St. Louis. Eight themed sections of the park reflect the region as the Gateway to the West.
Season: April – October
Hours: 10 am – Closing
Admission: Pay-One-Price
Parking: Daily charge

SIX FLAGS OVER TEXAS
I-30
Arlington, Texas 76004-0191, USA
(817) 640-8900
The original Six Flags park, named for the six different flags that have flown over the state of Texas throughout history. Themed areas of the park reflect those countries and contain scores of great rides and attractions, including the award-winning TEXAS GIANT wooden roller coaster, which is a favorite of many seasoned riders.
Season: March – December
Hours: 10 am – Closing
Admission: Pay-One-Price
Parking: Daily charge

STRATOSPHERE
2000 Las Vegas Blvd. South
Las Vegas, Nevada 89104, USA
(702) 383-4714
Dominating the skyline of Las Vegas, the 1149-foot tall Stratosphere Tower is the tallest free-standing observation tower in the United States. In addition to being utilized for sightseeing, eating and getting married, the tower supports two thrill rides on top: the HIGH ROLLER coaster (at the 909-foot plateau) and a Space Shot spanning the distance from 921 to 1101 feet above ground.
Season: Year-round
Parking: Free
(Hours and admission prices not available at publication time)

UNIVERSAL STUDIOS FLORIDA
1000 Universal Studios Plaza
Orlando, Florida 32819-7610, USA
(407) 363-8000
A 450-acre movie studio/theme park with a sister park in Universal City, California, Universal Studios contains some of the most technically-advanced simulator rides and attractions in the world. Here guests can "ride the movies" and experience films such as *Jaws*, *Earthquake*, *Back To The Future* and *Terminator 2* first-hand in an outstanding theme park atmosphere.
Season: Year-round
Hours: 10 am – 10 pm
Admission: Pay-One-Price
Parking: Daily charge

VALLEYFAIR!
One Valleyfair Drive (off Hwy. 101)
Shakopee, Minnesota 55379-3098, USA
(612) 445-7600
Six roller coasters including the WILD THING, standing more than 200 feet tall, an IMAX theater, three childrens areas, a waterpark section and dozens of other rides, attractions and entertainment combine to make Valleyfair! a very enjoyable place to take the family.
Season: May – September
Hours: 10 am – Closing
Admission: Pay-One-Price
Parking: Daily charge

WALT DISNEY WORLD
Routes 4 & 192
Lake Buena Vista,
Florida 32830-1000, USA
(407) 828-2100
The 35,000-acre Walt Disney World Resort encompasses 22 hotels, the Magic Kingdom, EPCOT Center and Disney-MGM Studios theme parks, four waterparks, Pleasure Island entertainment complex, campgrounds, wedding chapel, shopping and restaurants.
Season: Year-round
Hours: Various
(theme parks generally open at 10 am)
Admission (theme parks): Pay-One-Price
Parking (theme parks): Daily charge

WET 'N WILD
2601 Las Vegas Boulevard South
Las Vegas, Nevada 89119, USA
(702) 734-0088
The perfect way to cool off in the heat of the Las Vegas strip, this waterpark features all kinds of slides and chutes, a wave pool, a rapid river, and features a giant Children's Water Playground.
Season: April – September
Hours: 10am – 8pm
Admission: Pay-One-Price
Parking: Free

YOMIURI LAND
3294 Yanokuchi
Inagi
Tokyo 206, Japan
(81) 449661111
Located on the outskirts of metropolitan Tokyo, the popular Yomiuri Land amusement park and recreation complex offers more than thirty rides, including the longest and fastest coaster in Japan – the BANDIT, and the beautiful WHITE CANYON wood track coaster.
Season: Year-round
Hours: Various
Admission: Pay-One-Price; individual ride tickets

ACKNOWLEDGMENTS

The publishers would like to thank all the contributing parks for permission to reproduce photographs and logos. Also, thanks to those organizations and individuals who helped compile this volume, including:

Carolyn Boos, Paramount's Kings Island, Ohio
Sarah Dornford-May, Blackpool Pleasure Beach
Dana Hammontree, Knott's Berry Farm
Emma Hart, Chessington World Of Adventures
Andrew Hine, RCCGB
Janice Lifke and Robin Innes, Cedar Point
Linda Meyer, TOGO International
Pippa Paxton, Lightwater Valley
Nicky Springthorpe, Alton Towers
Susan Taylor, West Edmonton Mall
Mark Wijman, *Inside Track*

NOTES

Where available, the figures quoted in ride specifications are those of the constructors concerned. Ride times and speeds quoted for roller coasters may vary, depending on the season, weather and track conditions, time of day and weights of the riders.

Photography in this book has been undertaken with permission and supervision. Photography in unauthorised areas or on board rides could be dangerous and should not be attempted without the express permission of the park.

CLUBS and ORGANIZATIONS

There are a number of organizations which encourage education, preservation and enjoyment of amusement parks and their attractions. Most hold meetings, conventions and other gatherings throughout the year where park and ride aficionados can enjoy these thrill machines and interact with others having similar interests. For more information, write to:

AMERICAN COASTER ENTHUSIASTS (ACE)
PO Box 8226
Chicago, Illinois 60680
USA

MID-ATLANTIC COASTER CLUB (MACC)
7532 Murillo Street
Springfield, Virginia 22151
USA
(703) 569-5099

NATIONAL AMUSEMENT PARK HISTORICAL ASSOCIATION (NAPHA)
PO Box 83
Mt. Prospect, Illinois 60656
USA

ROLLER COASTER CLUB OF GREAT BRITAIN
PO Box 235
Uxbridge
Middlesex UB10 0TF
United Kingdom

WESTERN NEW YORK COASTER CLUB (WNYCC)
Rick Taylor – Membership Director
4731 Forest Grove
Fort Wayne, Indiana 46835
USA
(219) 486-4450

INSIDE TRACK

Inside Track
PO Box 7956
Newark, Delaware, USA 19714-7956
24-hour telephone: (302) 737 3667

Inside Track is the only publication of its kind in the world, recognized as the one-stop source for amusement industry news, current and future ride installations, interviews with key industry personnel, updates on memorabilia and collectibles, special events, and more. *IT* is available by subscription from the address above.